Date Due

NOV 1 0 1981			
NOV 1 2 1981			
MAY 1 0 1985			
MAR 2 1 1991			
FS 3/93			
MAR 0 3 1994			
3/22/96 -ILL			
NOV 0 4 1996			
MAR 0 6 2002			
			JE '73

D-DAYS AT DAYTON

D-DAYS

AT DAYTON

Reflections on the Scopes Trial

Edited by
Jerry R. Tompkins

LOUISIANA STATE UNIVERSITY PRESS   Baton Rouge/1965

Copyright © *1965 by*
Louisiana State University Press

Library of Congress Catalogue Card Number 65-24677
Manufactured in the United States of America by
Parthenon Press, Nashville, Tennessee

Designed by Jules B. McKee

PREFACE

I N July, 1925, John Thomas Scopes, a young schoolteacher in Dayton, Tennessee, was convicted of teaching the theory of evolution, a crime which had been forbidden (and still is) by state law since the previous March. To the public, the trial was primarily a courtroom conflict between a leading fundamentalist and former presidential candidate, William Jennings Bryan, as prosecuting attorney, and a famous agnostic and champion of the underdog, Clarence Darrow, as chief counsel for the defense. Scopes himself did not even testify. He gave his name to the historic episode and then quickly passed into obscurity.

Some thirty years later, while reading a review of the Broadway play *Inherit the Wind,* I noted that the real-life counterpart of the play's young teacher-hero, John T. Scopes, was then living somewhere in Louisiana. Since I resided in Louisiana at that time myself, I was overwhelmed by curiosity. Where in the state was he living? What had happened in those intervening years to the man who had been the figurehead, if not the central figure, of one of the world's most famous trials?

Investigation revealed that since 1940 John Scopes had lived quietly in Shreveport—barely a twenty-minute drive from the town where I had attended high school. I at once resolved to meet this man of oblivion, though it was some years before I had the opportunity. Our first meeting occurred late in 1962 and was repeated on a number of subsequent occasions. The idea of a book grew out of those visits, but was not due to any suggestion from Scopes himself; indeed, the information contained here in the brief Scopes profile

v

was given only at my earnest request, for John Scopes is a man who lives in the present rather than in the past. Not dependent upon his 1925 fame for a satisfying self-image, he is today the acme of modesty, more interested in discussing current political and social issues than in talking about himself. Yet he is a person who was remarkably prepared by certain emotional, intellectual, and social factors for his role at Dayton—perhaps for a far greater role than he chose to play.

The purpose of the present volume is to examine certain aspects of the Dayton trial in the light of subsequent history. My intention in the Scopes profile, for example, is to provide some insight into the personal dynamics that produced John T. Scopes as the "man of the hour" in 1925. The value and purpose of Scopes's own essay is to be found in its focus on certain personalities and incidents of the trial as he, the defendant, viewed and understood them.

Scopes does not write from the perspective of the general of an army, or even that of a military historian, who might outline in bold strokes the overall strategy, the long-range goals, or the reflective, analytical evaluation of a certain battle. Rather, he writes as a soldier involved as both participant and observer. For a combat soldier, certain personalities are remembered vividly, humorous or tragic incidents recalled with a sense of personal involvement, and yet a comprehensive assessment of what is happening is not evident. Of course, John Scopes in 1925 was young and inexperienced. But just as a general can fight no battles without soldiers, so neither Darrow nor Bryan, nor for that matter any of the issues, could have had the world for an audience except for John Scopes.

Part II of this volume is an account of "The Monkey Trial"—the nickname coined because of the evolutionists' theory that "man and the anthropoid apes must have branched off from a common stock." While the trial was reported by over a hundred newspapermen, none was better known than H. L. Mencken, columnist for the Baltimore *Evening Sun* and the spokesman for the "lost generation" of neo-intellectuals. The irreverent, cutting wit with which he reported the trial was typical of his assessment of beliefs and values which, in the 1920's, were already undergoing radical change. We are far enough removed from the period, however, to appreciate these classic excerpts of reporting.

The Scopes trial spawned conflict and discussion on several issues: the right of taxpayers to control what is taught in public schools, the practical nature of the concept of the separation of church and state, the risks of academic freedom, and the tension between religion and science. This volume is concerned with the latter two issues, as they are viewed by various writers, some of whom were participants in the trial.

The initiating issue of the trial was the threat to academic freedom which the American Civil Liberties Union, headed by Roger Baldwin, saw in the Tennessee Anti-Evolution Act. This organization was largely responsible for the case being pressed. Mr. Baldwin's chapter presents the development of the case as it was planned in its pre-Dayton stages by the A.C.L.U. and his evaluation of the impact of the trial on the issue of academic freedom in the last forty years.

Although never permitted to testify, the scientists called to Dayton by the defense made an important educational impact on the public through their statements released to the press. Instrumental in distributing these reports was Watson Davis, who here tells of the part he played. Winterton C. Curtis, Kirtley F. Mather, and LaMont C. Cole (both Curtis and Mather were present at the trial) review the scientific affidavits submitted to the Dayton court in the light of new knowledge gained in the past forty years. These affidavits have held up surprisingly well with many of their assumptions becoming further substantiated.

Theology, however, has taken a new direction. In 1925 there was hardly a theological stance outside of a brittle fundamentalism on the one hand and an uneasy and uncertain liberalism on the other. Even liberal theology was unprepared to deal with the challenge which evolutionary science thrust forth. But, today there are possibilities for a new science-theology dialogue. The new posture in theological thinking is explored here by John Dillenberger and Carlyle Marney.

Despite the increasing amity, the tensions remain. In October, 1964, the Texas State Textbook Committee heard the complaints of various individuals against the use of textbooks which present evolution as an established fact. The committee also reviewed letters submitted by textbook publishers defending the accounts on evolution found in their respective texts.[1] As other writers in this volume

---

1 See "39 Years Later, Monkey Law Still on the Books," *Arkansas Gazette,* October 8, 1964. In November the textbook committee ruled in favor of the publishers and their textbooks.

indicate, this phenomenon, resurgent in only the last year or so, is evident in several states today.

Ultimately, however, there is a deeper problem which cannot be limited to a fundamentalist complaint; it is, to some extent, a tension known to millions—a tension not merely sectarian, but universal. As Walter Lippmann, in commenting upon presidential candidate Barry Goldwater's reference to "a virtual despair" being evident among masses of Americans, has said:

> [This "virtual despair"] is the unease of the old Adam who is not ready for the modern age. The malady is caused, I believe, by the impact of science upon religious certainty and of technological progress upon the settled order of family, class and community. The virtual despair comes from being uprooted, homeless, naked, alone and unled. It comes from being lost in a universe where the meaning of life and of the social order are no longer given from on high and transmitted from the ancestors but have to be invented and discovered and experimented with, each lonely individual for himself. . . . the poignant question, which is as yet not answered, is how, with the ancestral order dissolved and the ancient religious certainties corroded by science, the modern man can find meanings which bind his experience and engage his faculties and his passions. Two centuries ago the conservative could still believe that he could preserve the old regime and the ancient certainties. If he thinks so today he is a romantic and deluded reactionary.[2]

The tension between science and religion is real and permanent. Indeed, the only period in which this tension was momentarily relieved is to be found in primitive history—and in an unlikely personage—*the witch doctor.* He was the primitive's answer to the problem of bridging the world seen and the world unseen, the natural and the supernatural. And, indeed, it was a perfectly logical arrangement; he was both physician and priest, scientist and theologian. All questions of origin and destiny, of essence and function, or extensions and limitations were gathered into this one functionary; and if he was incomprehensible, he at least reduced the painful tension between man's two worlds, the natural and supernatural.

With the passing of time all orders change. The witch doctor surrendered his *mysterium tremendum* to successors. But the successors were specialists, scientists and theologians. And in these two, even now, is symbolized the splitness of man himself—social and

---

2 Walter Lippmann, "Today and Tomorrow," *Washington Post,* August 4, 1964. (Used with permission of the author.)

individuate—forever related and forever separated; *gnosis* (knowledge) and *pistis* (faith), and both in search of a convincing final authority. The quest does not end.

But today science and theology have been shorn of much of their provincialism. We no longer dwell in neat, well-defined and separate entrenchments, taking potshots at one another on every occasion. Both are essential—*of essence*—to reality. We have entered into dialogue. We are hearing and being heard.

J.R.T.

Monticello, Arkansas

ACKNOWLEDGMENTS

A NY editor is hard pressed to thank all who help produce what he may selfishly call *his* book. In the case of this volume, the contributing writers not only made the undertaking possible but are to be thanked for having made the work keenly enjoyable. Among them, Kirtley F. Mather graciously assisted me in editing several of the papers. John Scopes, who gave numerous afternoons and evenings over a two-year period to answering endless questions, has become a friend rather than a project or historical relic; his wife Mildred shared scrapbooks and mementos which helped me sense the atmosphere, geographically and socially, that pervaded the time of the trial. The vigorous personal correspondence that developed between the senior member of our group, Winterton C. Curtis, and myself is eclipsed only by his packets of pictures, cards, and other surprises sent to and enjoyed by our children.

I am indebted to Thomas C. Coleman, chairman of the division of language and literature at Arkansas A. & M. College, Monticello, Arkansas, and to James A. Wharton, assistant professor of Bible at Austin Presbyterian Theological Seminary, Austin, Texas, for reading the first drafts of several chapters and making helpful suggestions.

Various members of the Arkansas A. & M. library staff have assisted me in securing books and microfilms from other parts of the country.

Shelby T. McCloy, professor of history; Charles F. Elton, dean of admissions and registrar; Kathryn W. Shelburne, assistant dean of admissions and registrar; and Mary Hester Cooper of the university archives—all of the University of Kentucky, Lexington— were helpful in gathering background material for the Scopes profile.

Virginia Seguine, librarian at Bryan College, Dayton, Tennessee, secured photographs and assisted in proofreading parts of the manuscript.

Dorothy C. Clair rendered valuable service in organizing and refining the final manuscript.

Marie Arnold, Mary Jo Barnett, Joanne Gowan, and Carra Nell Tilley have been faithful typists as well as encouraging friends.

My wife Marcia has patiently endured my preoccupation with manuscripts and letters and has offered only encouragement since the beginning of the project. Any eloquent word of thanks would fall far short of my just debt to her.

No doubt there are others who deserve more than my silence. The fallibility of the human memory rather than any lack of gratitude accounts for names which, belatedly, will be remembered.

CONTENTS

ILLUSTRATIONS

following page 32

D·DAYS AT DAYTON

The Tennessee Anti-Evolution Act

Chapter 27, House Bill 185 (By Mr. Butler) Public Acts of Tennessee for 1925

AN ACT prohibiting the teaching of the Evolution Theory in all the Universities, Normals and all other public schools of Tennessee, which are supported in whole or in part by the public school funds of the State, and to provide penalties for the violations thereof.

Section 1. BE IT ENACTED BY THE GENERAL ASSEMBLY OF THE STATE OF TENNESSEE, That it shall be unlawful for any teacher in any of the Universities, Normals and all other public schools of the State which are supported in whole or in part by the public school funds of the State, to teach any theory that denies the story of the Divine Creation of man as taught in the Bible, and to teach instead that man has descended from a lower order of animals.

Section 2. BE IT FURTHER ENACTED, That any teacher found guilty of the violation of this Act, shall be guilty of a misdemeanor and upon conviction, shall be fined not less than One Hundred ($100.00) Dollars nor more than Five Hundred ($500.00) Dollars for each offense.

Section 3. BE IT FURTHER ENACTED, That this Act take effect from and after its passage, the public welfare requiring it.

Passed March 13, 1925
(W. F. Barry),
Speaker of the House of Representatives.
(L. D. Hill),
Speaker of the Senate.
Approved March 21, 1925.
(Austin Peay),
Governor.

The State of Tennessee v. John Thomas Scopes

On July 10, 1925, the circuit court of Rhea County, Tennessee, opened the case of *The State of Tennessee* v. *John Thomas Scopes* with Judge John T. Raulston presiding.

Counsel for the Prosecution:

William Jennings Bryan, three-times Democratic candidate for President

"Gen'l" Ben McKenzie, district attorney and a practicing lawyer in Dayton for thirty-two years

J. Gordon McKenzie, his son and county judge

Sue and Herbert Hicks, young Dayton attorneys

A. T. Stewart, circuit attorney general

William Jennings Bryan, Jr., Los Angeles attorney

Counsel for the Defense:

Clarence Darrow, criminal lawyer of Chicago

John R. Neal, former dean of the University of Tennessee Law School at Knoxville

Arthur Garfield Hays, New York attorney

Dudley Field Malone, New York attorney and former Collector of the Port of New York

W. O. Thompson, New York attorney

F. B. McElwee, attorney

On July 21, 1925, the jury found the defendant guilty as charged.

PART ONE

SCOPES

A boy, twenty-one [twenty-four] years old, had come from Kentucky and applied for a position as teacher in the high school. His name was John T. Scopes. And he was destined to become famous. . . . he was indicted for the crime of teaching the truth. John T. Scopes was not the first man indicted for this most heinous offense. So far as I know, he was the last, up to the present time.

CLARENCE DARROW
The Story of My Life

JOHN THOMAS SCOPES: *A Profile*

JERRY R. TOMPKINS

J ERRY R. TOMPKINS, minister of the First Presbyterian
Church of Monticello, Arkansas, received his B.A. in political
science from Austin College before attending the Austin Presbyterian
Theological Seminary. He became interested in the Dayton trial
because of the theological-scientific tension that it exposed but did
not resolve. His first meeting with John Scopes, the focal figure of
the trial, was in 1962; the ensuing friendship resulted in this volume.

November, 1962

I wait in the Shreveport office of John T. Scopes while a recep-
tionist tries to find him. No mementos of the Dayton days are on the
walls or desk. Finally the door opens.

Forty-year-old pictures are misleading. Gone are the smooth-faced
boyish look, the horn-rimmed glasses, the shock of reddish hair. The
man I see is that John T. Scopes—plus the years. Now his face is
weatherbeaten from years outdoors, and the wrinkles confirm his
sixty-two years. He is slightly stooped. His suit is casually worn, and
he holds a cigarette—an item he is seldom seen without. He smiles
and one sees immediately why Edward R. Murrow spoke of him as
having been "a rather personable young school teacher . . . "[1] He
invites me to sit down.

1 Edward R. Murrow, "I Can Hear It Now," Vol. III (Columbia Records,
1950).

I try to begin, not knowing how he really feels about Dayton, his
life, his disappointments, the defeats he has known. Above all not
knowing how he feels about the oblivion that enveloped him within a
year after the trial. I express my gratitude for his giving of his
time. Then, in a warm, fatherly tone he says, "Well, I'm deeply
flattered that you wanted to come by and visit me."

I discover he has not wasted time thinking about the trial. I speak
of persons I have read about in connection with the trial; he isn't
sure he remembers them. I recall things he said at the time of the
trial; yes, he remembers that . . . but he'd forgotten that was the
way he had said it. It is not a matter of bad memory; it is a matter
of what John Scopes has considered important, and soon it becomes
apparent that there are important things to him that go back beyond
1925 and the trial, back to 1883 and the arrival in the United States
of his father. . . .

The twenty-three-year-old Englishman walked down the gang-
plank gazing at the frontier skyline of Galveston, Texas. Among his
few belongings, the young immigrant carried four treasured volumes:
a Bible and a Church of England hymnbook given him by his mother,
a copy of Thomas Carlyle's *The French Revolution,* and the fourth,
Charles Darwin's *Origin of Species,* published only a year before
this young man's birth in 1860. He did not know then that many in
the United States considered this book contraband, nor could he have
known that forty years later this book would play a significant role
in the life of his only son. The disembarking passenger was Thomas
Scopes.

Scopes was to work for various midwestern railroads for over
forty years, sometimes as a fireman or roundhouse foreman, but
usually as a machinist. Politically he was a Socialist, and, although he
did not join the American Railroad Union strike of 1894, he was
greatly impressed with the ideas of his friend and fellow-employee
Eugene V. Debs, the mind and spirit of the strike. Shortly after the
strike, Scopes became active in the railroad union and later helped
organize a machinists' union. The preamble of that union's constitution was largely the result of the thought and pen of Thomas
Scopes.

Although he earned his livelihood by manual skills, his intellectual
interests were keen, partly because he had been tutored as a child by
a family friend who made his fine library available to young Scopes.

Scopes's interests ran mainly to political and natural sciences, but he and his wife Mary, whom he had met and married during his first year in the United States, encouraged their children to develop interests in a wider range of subjects. Greek philosophy, Shakespeare, and the more contemporary writers such as Charles Dickens and Mark Twain were a part of the literature to which the Scopes children were consistently exposed. The children—three of whom became teachers—were frequently questioned on their reading by their parents.

Thomas Scopes was an agnostic, but never an atheist. He dutifully joined the church of his wife's heritage, the Presbyterian church, and served as an officer for a time.

On August 3, 1900, Mary Scopes gave birth to her fifth child and only son, John Thomas Scopes. After four daughters, the new son was received wholeheartedly by the entire family—an acceptance that John T. Scopes would consider a most important influence throughout his life.

John attended the schools in the town of his birth, Paducah, Kentucky—first the old Washington School and later the Lone Oak School following the moving of the Scopes family to a house outside the city limits.

In 1911, Thomas Scopes moved his family to Danville, Illinois, where young John continued his education until another move in 1916, when he was completing the ninth grade, took the family to Salem, Illinois. Here the boy was exposed to his first courses in the sciences—an experience considerably enhanced by stimulating teachers who apparently accepted Darwin's theories. Scopes liked geology but was indifferent to botany.

Ecclesiastically existing somewhere between his father's unbaptized idealism and his mother's Calvinism, John was exposed to various Protestant churches as he matured, but evidenced no particular zeal for the tenets of any faith. The most decisive of these church relationships centered about a men's Bible class he attended during his senior year in high school at Salem.

The teacher was young, attractive, well educated, and successful in business. But he proved to be unacceptable to John who, though fast becoming an agnostic, felt that there should be some consistency between what a man professed and how he lived. The teacher in question created the problem by referring to the partying on weekends in Chicago hotels, while Scopes sat pondering what his elders were saying about the unreasonably low wages being paid the girls working in this man's small manufacturing company and how this fact might in some way be related to the increase in prostitution in the town. Scopes was bold enough to make reference in class one Sunday to this inconsistent state of affairs; shortly thereafter, it was suggested that he might try some of the other churches. Except for rare and special occasions, this marked the end of John Scopes's sojourn with the church.

Entering the University of Illinois at Urbana in 1919, Scopes pursued a major in chemistry. However, some of the chemicals with which he worked irritated his bronchial tubes and there followed some months under the care of a doctor. With the end of the school term he gave up the study of chemistry.

Since the family planned to move back to Paducah upon Thomas Scopes's retirement, it seemed wise for John to transfer to the University of Kentucky in 1920.

It was a notable era for the University of Kentucky. In the post-World War I decade, the university was striving for excellence —a goal that could be achieved only with the help of a friendly state legislature. To aid their own, the Lexington Board of Commerce in February, 1922, invited the state legislature to the campus at Lexington. The purpose of the invitation was, of course, promotional and was directly related to the hope of a larger appropriation for the university from the 1922 legislative session. During the same session, an anti-evolution bill was introduced which, to some university supporters, apparently threatened the hope of favored treatment for the university. The president of the university, Frank L. McVey, publicly denied any "connection between the agitation about evolution and the chances for greater financial support"; [2] in any case, the legislature favored an expansion of the university and, in the same year, defeated the anti-evolution bill. "Do Your Own Thinking" had been President McVey's theme in his semi-annual "Between-us Day" message to students and faculty; and Professor W. D. Funkhouser, Scopes's zoology professor, who believed in doing his own thinking, taught the theory of evolution. Neither the university administration nor the state legislature saw fit to stop him.

Thus John was taught Darwin's theory in the unfettered freedom of Kentucky's classrooms. He took it to be a normal part of learning

2 *Kentucky Kernel* (student weekly), February 11, 1922.

contemporary biology. His course of study at the University of Kentucky, interrupted several semesters because of his recurring bronchial ailment, was primarily in the physical sciences; however, the transcript of his college record reveals no lack of subject balance. During the academic year 1923-24, he completed twenty-four hours of credit in the College of Law, and in June, 1924, he received his bachelor's degree in Arts-Law.

Upon completing college, John Scopes assumed he would be hired by some Kentucky school as coach and science teacher. This might have happened except for the fact that in the Tennessee River Valley town of Dayton, Tennessee, the man who had been coach and physics teacher had taken another job at the last minute. The school board was desperate, but not for long. An easygoing, quiet John Scopes was happy to be of service.

Within a short time, John was well known and liked in Dayton. He was considered a man who could be trusted in the classroom as well as on the athletic field. He was occasionally seen at the Cumberland Presbyterian Church, particularly on those Sunday evenings when he and a friend would be looking for a couple of dates. Scopes was noted for being helpful and obliging when others needed him; for example, he was glad to substitute for the regular biology teacher for two weeks in April, 1925, when the latter became ill. The month before, the Tennessee legislature had passed the Butler Act, an anti-evolution bill, making it illegal for any teacher in a school supported wholly or partly by state funds to teach a theory of man's descent from a lower order of animals.

George Hunter's *A Civic Biology,* the textbook used by the biology class in which Scopes substituted, had been in use in the Dayton Schools since 1919 and was annually dispensed through the Textbook Department of Robinson's Drug Store. It commended the Darwinian theory of the origin of species with nonchalant candor. Scopes did not question this position for it seemed like standard fare for modern high school biology; after all, this was precisely what he had been taught in high school and college. In fact, no one in Dayton questioned it. Most people knew about the Butler Act passed the month before, but nothing that Dayton science teachers had given out in lectures in the school had seemed to hurt anyone.

Meanwhile in New York, the secretary of the American Civil Liberties Union (A.C.L.U.), Lucile Milner, had seen a small news item which told of the governor signing the Butler Act on March 21.

She showed it to Roger Baldwin, director of the A.C.L.U., who promptly obtained his board's backing for the raising of a special fund to finance a test case.[3] News of the fund was picked up by newspapers all over the country.

In Dayton, George Rappleyea, as he read the news of the A.C.L.U.'s offer in his newspaper, was the first person to seriously consider making Dayton the center of the test case. Rappleyea was thirty-one years of age, a native of New York, and at that time manager and engineer for the Cumberland Coal and Iron Company. His motives were obscure, or at least mixed. But this much seems to have been true: Rappleyea was personally opposed to the Butler Act and was eager to have Dayton "put on the map." To what extent he hoped that the town's anticipated fame would result in new capital being invested in the area—some of which might save the almost defunct Cumberland Coal and Iron Company—has been a matter of conjecture. The company was later dissolved. That Dayton was "put on the map" is a matter of history.

When Rappleyea presented the idea of asking a Dayton teacher to serve as protagonist in a test case to F. E. Robinson, president of the school board and a local druggist, both men agreed that John T. Scopes was the most likely candidate. He was young and without a family; thus any unforeseen unpleasant consequences probably would not have long-range effects. Furthermore, the townspeople already knew that Scopes was opposed to the new law.

As the two men talked, one or two others joined them, each agreeing that the test case probably would hurt no one and that it would likely help Dayton. Mr. Robinson asked two high school boys, at that moment sipping an after-school soda pop at his fountain, if they would mind going back to the school and asking Mr. Scopes to come to the drug store. The boys were glad to do it.

Arriving at the drug store, John Scopes found himself in the midst of a lively discussion about evolution. After listening a few minutes he remarked that he did not see how it was possible for anyone to teach biology without considering Darwin's theory. Rappleyea's elated reply was that apparently Scopes had already violated the law during the two weeks in which he had substitute-taught the biology class. As a matter of fact, Scopes on April 23 had assigned the chapter which included a discussion of the doctrine of evolution, the evolution of

3 Ray Ginger, *Six Days or Forever?* (Boston: Beacon Press, 1958), 21.

man, and Darwin's theory of natural selection. Ironically, Scopes was sick himself on April 24, and the class recitation never took place. He had, however, taught the theory in his general science classes.

The strategy which Rappleyea had already worked out consisted mostly of Scopes agreeing to stand trial; others—such as civic promoters, newsmen, and the American Civil Liberties Union—would do the rest. Even his "arrest" for the crime would consist solely of Robinson's calling a reporter in Chattanooga to report Scopes's violation. Scopes agreed to be the man of the hour.

To some extent, obviously, Scopes was used by others for ulterior motives. But to say that this was the nature of Scopes's involvement is to ignore the personality of the man himself. He now took the matter seriously. "It was evident," said Clarence Darrow seven years after the trial, "that Scopes was trying to do for Dayton, Tennessee, what Socrates did for Athens." [4] Darrow's statement is excessive, but it is true that Scopes was acting consistently with his parental background, for now the values of Thomas Scopes became evident as never before. The elder Scopes's high regard for education, for freedom of inquiry, and his cautious agnosticism in regard to dogma—friendly to religion but never committed to it—had converged in the personality of his son John to create the ideal defendant.

But the personality of John Scopes was not for gaudy displays of sensationalism nor was he built for dramatic fighting for his own rights or even for the rights of others. He felt strongly about the new state law, but he did not feel that his academic freedom was being restricted in Dayton. His school board granted him maximum freedom, a fact which John Scopes felt was, after all, the most important thing. He did not criticize another school board that might feel differently. He did object, however, to the state telling *all* Tennessee schools what could or could not be taught. This he felt tended to make people all think alike, a situation that stifles free and open discussion.

Preparations began in Dayton as well as at A.C.L.U. headquarters in New York. Finally, Scopes was invited to New York to hear what the A.C.L.U. actually planned to do. He was offered alternatives in choosing an attorney. He chose Clarence Darrow, the nation's best-known defense lawyer, who had already offered his services without fee. Earlier Scopes had employed John R. Neal, a law school professor from Knoxville. Neal was to continue as a Scopes counsel.

4 Clarence Darrow, *The Story of My Life* (New York: Scribner's, 1932), 261.

Dudley Field Malone and Arthur Garfield Hays would assist Darrow
in the defense. "For the first, the last, the only time in my life," said
Darrow later, "I volunteered my services in a case . . . because I
really wanted to take part in it." [5] Said Scopes of Darrow and
Malone: "I know of no two lawyers in the country who are more
capable of defending a great cause than Mr. Darrow and Mr.
Malone." [6]

The trial began on July 10. At no time was John T. Scopes a
central figure; in fact, he was not even called to testify during the
trial. Bryan and Darrow were by far the commanding personalities.
Partly because of this shift of the pivotal point, it was impossible for
Scopes to sense any great personal involvement in the trial itself. He
could not feel the uncompromising sense of purpose, for example, that
held Luther together at Worms, nor did he know any urge to proclaim a new Truth such as that which set Copernicus at the center
of controversy that raged for at least a generation. Scopes did not
see himself embarking on a life-long labor calculated to deliver a
new concept of education in the tenacious style of a John Dewey.
Although Scopes was utterly sincere and committed, neither the
situation that emerged during the trial nor his own temperament
would permit him the roles of either an embattled hero or a venerable
martyr. When Dayton and the trial were finally behind him, Scopes
would never again be involved in any significant way in the gigantic
issues that had stormed about him for eight days in the summer of
1925.

On July 21, the case of *The State of Tennessee* v. *John Thomas
Scopes* ended in a conviction. Scopes was fined $100 but otherwise
was a free man.

The convicted defendant John T. Scopes was tired. He had wit-
nessed the smashing of his hope of a dignified court proceeding as
the giants, Darrow and Bryan, a sensation-starved press, and a
curious world perverted the issues into a circus. Friendly, shy Scopes
was sick of the whole mess.

Now he faced one of the major decisions of his life: where was
he to go from here? The Dayton school board, with mixed feelings
about the fame into which the town was thrust by the trial, offered
Scopes his old job. But he knew that teaching in Dayton could never
be the same again. There were numerous other opportunities includ-

5   *Ibid.*, 244.
6   Ginger, *Six Days or Forever?*, 69.

ing lecture tours and a movie contract. Thirty-nine years later Scopes would say, "I knew that none of these offers—motion pictures, lectures, writing 'my' story—could give me two things I wanted above all else: peace and emotional stability."

The future was already decided. Watson Davis, reporter for Science Service at Washington, thought science owed a debt of gratitude to John Scopes. And what could be more appropriate than a gift from scientists and newsmen of a scholarship to the university whose professors were the most responsive in aiding the late defense, namely, the University of Chicago? Scopes gratefully accepted the scholarship and began his studies in September, 1925.

The university was sympathetic toward the now famous young man. All but declaring him "officially unavailable," the university offered Scopes what he was now ready for, an opportunity to become a competent geologist. He became so engrossed in his studies that the A.C.L.U. and his attorneys were largely unsuccessful in renewing his interest in his case when it came before the Tennessee Supreme Court on appeal the next year. In January, 1927, the Tennessee Supreme Court reversed the Dayton court's decision but without Scopes ever having returned to Tennessee.

In May, 1927, John T. Scopes completed two years of graduate study in geology at the University of Chicago, was promptly hired by Gulf Oil of South America and sent to Venezuela. Scopes began the kind of work he came to love most, geological field work. In late 1928 he began to suffer from a form of blood poisoning, which forced him to return to the United States on January 1, 1929.

Leaving his job with Gulf, he took his father back to his native England. Thomas Scopes was now approaching seventy, and it was to be his only trip back home. After several months of pleasant visiting with relatives and old friends, they sailed for New York. The younger Scopes was barely off the boat when the Gulf office reached him by telephone asking him to return to Venezuela immediately.

In spite of his continuing fatigue from his former sojourn in Venezuela, he accepted. He spent six months at Lake Maracaibo, then moved to Ciudad Bolívar in the Orinoco basin. After a short time there, he went up the Orinoco River in a sailboat to Colombia. He ate, slept, and worked in the boat since the river had flooded the entire area. This proved to be a fascinating trip but accomplished little for Gulf's geological survey interests.

It was on this second tour of Venezuela, in 1930, that Scopes met and married his wife Mildred, daughter of an American businessman living in Venezuela. As a part of his commitment in marriage, Scopes was baptized in the Roman Catholic Church in Venezuela. It is the only church to which Scopes has had any formal relationship.

In September, 1930, he returned to the University of Chicago for a third and last year of study in geology. Scopes renewed his friendship with the Darrows in whose home he and his bride were frequently dinner guests. With the country deep in the Depression, the Scopeses spent the remainder of 1931 and 1932 living with his parents at Paducah while waiting for a new job opportunity.

The job did come, this time with United Gas Corporation. As company geologist in the Houston area he did reserve studies, the investigation of oil reservoir conditions. He continued this type of geological work after his transfer to the new company headquarters at Shreveport in 1940 and until his retirement in 1963.

November, 1962

Darkness has come. I express concern at keeping Scopes from dinner. He motions for me to sit down again, saying that his wife is away this evening and he is not expected home at any particular time. I relax again as in the company of an old friend.

We speak of many other things . . . geology, United Gas, his sons . . . to whom he has never told the story of the trial except as they have asked questions . . . Clarence Darrow, William Jennings Bryan, the witnesses. He is willing to discuss it . . . any of it. But he seeks to prove no points, does not brag, does not sentimentalize. It is as if he left Dayton and all that had happened to him there without bitterness or gratitude and moved on to something totally different.

John Thomas Scopes, like the citizen-soldier, defended an idea in time of crisis and then went contentedly to a quieter life, possessing the ability to walk away from center stage.

It has been said that John Scopes withdrew, refused interviews, would not talk about the trial. It is not so. He merely ignored public acclaim. Neither hostile nor self-seeking in his hour of public appraisal, he was content to let the hour of fame pass without regrets.

REFLECTIONS—*Forty Years After*

JOHN THOMAS SCOPES

IF I had been asked the last day of the trial what had been accomplished, I would have been a most embarrassed lad. Another
question that would have been hard to answer was why I had been
the defendant. For two good reasons I could not have answered
either question.

In the first place the general files were kept in New York; the
keepers of these files were the only ones who had knowledge of all
pretrial conferences and of the work preparatory to the presentation
of the case for the defense. I was in Tennessee or Kentucky most of
that time; many conferences were held and work was done that I
did not know about then and have no knowledge of today. I am
certain that the general files would disclose the thinking and the
real hopes of the many people who actively worked for the defense.
I believe, too, that these files would reveal that the defense had on its
side all of the facts, logic, and justice, but these weapons are often
ineffective in a battle against bigotry and prejudice.

Secondly, various aspects of the trial changed so completely from
what I had anticipated that I could not have given an intelligent
answer to anything even as simple as what effect all this had on one
John Scopes. The rapidity of events and resulting excitement did
not create favorable conditions for critical analysis. It was many
years later when Dayton, the trial, and Scopes were almost forgotten
and after I had reestablished myself as an ordinary citizen, that I
was able to form any conclusion as to the effects of the trial. I could
see even then, of course, that my situation was the strange result
of a long series of apparently unrelated events.

It was by pure chance that I had the particular ancestors I had and the good fortune to be born and become a member of my particular family. By the same token, had not a temporary health problem caused me to transfer at the beginning of my second year in college from the University of Illinois to the University of Kentucky, I probably would have become a permanent resident in Illinois and thus would not have been available for participation in the Dayton trial. If the man who had been coach and instructor in algebra and physics had not received a better offer and resigned a few days before Rhea County High School opened for the 1924–25 term, I probably would not ever have heard of Dayton. I was the first applicant with the proper qualifications who came to the attention of the school board, and, due to the emergency, the board offered me the job which I promptly accepted. Then, nine months later and at the age of twenty-four, I was the defendant in a case destined to attract worldwide attention.

The first or second day after the Associated Press had carried the story of my "arrest," John R. Neal, an able and well-known attorney from Knoxville, appeared in Dayton. I was informed by someone that a man at the hotel wanted to meet me and have an informal chat. As I entered the hotel, someone called out, "Mr. Neal, that's John Scopes entering the front door." Neal introduced himself and asked me if I had time to talk with him. That day, May 14, I engaged John R. Neal as my attorney.

We spent many hours together during the next two months, and at all times he was willing to discuss any problem of the pending case with me and to help ferret out all possible angles of any question, supplying me with all pertinent data he had at hand or knew of; but the final decision, he said, would have to be mine.

But Neal and I were really bystanders; for until the first part of June, all the defense policies and strategies were being worked out by the American Civil Liberties Union in New York. The only way Neal and I could obtain information was by reading it in the newspapers. But one thing became increasingly evident to our New York colleagues: Mr. Bryan's entry into the case as a special prosecuting attorney had thrown a monkey wrench in the gears of all their plans.

Finally, Neal and I were asked to come to New York for a series of conferences which were to last four or five days. The first day's meeting, though rather lengthy, mostly amounted to a briefing. All the activities and decisions up to that day were discussed. After that, except for the last day, all conferences were a rehash of our first meeting. Neal said very little, but I am certain that he concluded, as I had, that the group was stalling. It also appeared to me that they were afraid I would give them some kind of trouble, which I was not about to do, of course, once I had committed myself.

At last we were told that a luncheon-conference was set for the next day. Interested parties from Washington, Philadelphia, New York, and Boston would be present and some major decisions would be made. Neal had some advance information, for when we had returned to our hotel he commented on what kind of showing the lawyers for the A.C.L.U. then handling the case would make in a state court of Tennessee. I had not met Bainbridge Colby, a New York lawyer who, like Bryan, had served as Secretary of State under Wilson, but I could not picture him in a Rhea County court proceeding. Charles Evans Hughes had already said that he would participate only on the U.S. Supreme Court level. Arthur Garfield Hays was a brilliant fighter, but there was too much talent developing on the side of the prosecution for him to handle the job by himself. Then there was Clarence Darrow.

There were about fifteen to twenty men and women at the luncheon. The seating arrangement placed me next to Dudley Field Malone, and, while we were eating, Malone concentrated on giving me the qualifications of Darrow.

Rodger Baldwin, director of the A.C.L.U., called the meeting to order. Several orders of business were taken up. The general business having been disposed of, Malone arose and, in words to this effect, said, "I am authorized by Mr. Clarence Darrow to offer his services as a defense counsel to the American Civil Liberties Union and to this steering committee for the Dayton case. He will pay all of his expenses and will not accept a fee. He guarantees to remain as an active counsel until a final decision has been reached. Speaking for myself, I, Dudley Field Malone, offer you the same proposition." The arguments that followed were spoken in a normal conversational tone of voice, but they were bitter. These were arguments—not discussions. Any vote taken during the first thirty or forty minutes would have gone against Darrow two to one.

Malone, Father John Ryan, or Forrest Bailey—I am not sure who —suggested that it might be a good idea for the defendant and his counsel to express themselves on this issue. As well as I can remember, Neal did not express himself on the question of Darrow; rather, he spoke on the matter of venue, saying that he did not believe the federal district judge would take the case out of the state courts. It was a case of violation of a state law, he said, and the state courts would be given a chance to clean up their own back yard. As to the other points under consideration, concluded Neal, the defendant would have to speak for himself.

I had tried to follow the arguments as closely as possible. I did gather that the main problem was that some felt that Darrow was a headline chaser, and as a consequence the real issue would be obscured. If Darrow were injected into the case, the trial would become a carnival and any possible dignity in the fight for liberties would be lost. All this would mean that the money and effort already expended would be a total loss and any hope of getting a change of venue to the federal district court would fade.

Now it was my turn to speak. I pointed out to the group that if they thought that Darrow would have too much influence on the course of events, then they had forgotten apparently that William Jennings Bryan was himself a well-known national figure. The major headlines and news stories had already begun to drop the issues and to play up Mr. Bryan. As to creating a carnival atmosphere, my hearers should have been in Dayton the day Neal and I had left to come to New York. There was not enough room in that part of Tennessee to accommodate any more medicine men, traveling evangelists, and screwballs than were already there. If the carnival atmosphere and the shift in the tenor of the news stories from Dayton meant the loss of all our efforts up until now, then they were lost already. We could thank Mr. William Jennings Bryan for the loss. Furthermore, I felt that any member of the present legal staff should have the privilege of appearing at Dayton, if he should so choose. They should be kept available, I said, if and when the case were moved into the federal courts. I pointed out that we should continue to exert effort to obtain a change of venue, while recognizing that for the time being we were faced with a rough battle in the state courts. I concluded by stating that I would like to have Darrow and Malone join the battle in our behalf.

The conversations resumed, and every now and then one person would make a remark addressed to the entire group. The group finally decided to continue to work for a change of venue, to maintain the existing legal staff, and to leave to the discretion of each lawyer the matter of taking part in the proceedings at Dayton.

The hard core of opposition to Darrow as senior defense counsel died hard. One of them moved to accept Mr. Malone's offer but to shelve Mr. Darrow's offer until the next meeting of the steering committee. Malone was on his feet talking before the committeeman could finish his motion. He made it plain that if Darrow were not accepted, then he, Malone, would withdraw his own offer. The showdown had come. Mr. Darrow's proposition was put to a vote and his offer accepted—but just barely.

Neal and I arrived back in Dayton in time to attend a banquet given in honor of William Jennings Bryan. It had to be something special because the greatest man produced in the United States since the days of Thomas Jefferson was the honored guest. He had secured a house and, with his wife and son, moved in to live among the people of Dayton like any other citizen. He was sympathetic, kind, and understanding; he fraternized with everyone, even with the men who spent several months each year in the mountains making moonshine which they sold throughout the year. He was a staunch defender of their type of religion and never passed up an opportunity to occupy a pulpit and deliver a stirring sermon. He understood business—the local people knew a little about his interest in Florida real estate. Anything that was for the good of the common man he favored. He was indeed the Great Commoner.

The majority of the males over fifty years of age were proud to be able to say that on three different occasions their votes had been cast for him for the office of President. Those who had not voted for Bryan rationalized their position by saying that after all he was still a mortal and could not be right and perfect in everything.

I do not remember the location of the banquet hall, but it was spacious, large enough to seat all Daytonian males having the price of admission, the guest of honor, and all nonpaying deadheads, of which I was one. I remember there were windows on two sides of the hall. The people who did not have or would not part with the price of admission gathered outside at the windows so that they could listen to Bryan.

The last time I had seen Bryan was in 1919 when he delivered the commencement address at the Salem, Illinois, high school. I was a member of the graduating class. Bryan had met so many people that I could not believe it possible he would remember me, but as soon as everyone had found a place, Mr. Bryan came directly to me, shook hands, and asked how I was getting along. I responded by saying that I hoped he was enjoying good health. Then Bryan said, "John, we are on opposite sides this time. I hope we will not let that interfere in any way with our relationship." I said, "Mr. Bryan, everyone has the right to think in accordance with the way he sees things and to act accordingly. Believing differently on some issues should not influence the degree of respect and friendship one has for another." As he was taking his seat, he remarked, "Good, we shall get along fine."

I do not know if he actually remembered me, but it gave the Daytonians within hearing distance of the conversation something to talk about.

Bryan was a master at using mass psychology, and the wording and ideas of this speech were similar to those he had used on the several occasions I had been in his audience. A sentence out of one speech which I remembered and which he used again at Dayton, illustrates what I mean: "The world is made up of two kinds of people: those who are so busy producing they have no time to collect, and those who are so busy collecting they have no time to produce." He emphasized this idea at the banquet and sprinkled in a few pleas to get back to the old time religion. That pleased everybody. His delivery and gestures were a combination of a fighting political oration, a sermon, and a homey, fireside chat, with emphasis on the informal chat. As I looked around there was no doubt about the response of the Daytonians to Bryan's magnetism and ability to lead.

For several days almost every conversation I overheard or was a participant in hinged upon Bryan. He had the best judgment, was the smartest, the most religious; in short, he was the best in everything.

I began to wonder how Darrow would be received. My own standing in the community was the same before and after the banquet, but I could explain that by the fact that the community considered me as one of its own, and, too, Bryan had been very friendly with me.

To my great relief, Darrow, at least outwardly, was also welcomed with respect and friendship. To show they were impartial, Bryan's banquet was duplicated for Darrow. I was seated next to Darrow, but everything—the toastmaster, the menu, the hall, and the people inside and outside—was the same.

Darrow shook hands and exchanged pleasantries with each person at the speaker's table, but that was the last time during the banquet that he directed a remark to any one individual. Then, after the meal, people relaxed as Darrow began to speak. They were pleased to hear that their philosophies, ideas, and knowledge of various topics were of interest to him; besides, he asked questions and they had a chance to hear themselves talk—and all of us like to listen to ourselves. If anything developed that Darrow could use later, he remembered it.

Darrow's talk was entirely different from Bryan's. He did not tell them what to think, what to believe, nor offer any panaceas by which to lead them to greater glory and prosperity. It was not the speech of a crusader. He gave a short but humorous story of his life. He told of how he first became interested in the legal profession by reading law books to a blacksmith who also wished to become a lawyer. He and the blacksmith went to Indianapolis to take the bar examination. At 4:00 P.M. on the day of the examination, a fresh round of drinks was ordered and downed in one gulp. Then, the chairman of the examining board informed them that they had passed the examination. Darrow told the audience that for two years he had practiced law in a tin shop (the local tinner was the justice of the peace) and played poker on the side. He nearly starved. Then, he started playing poker and practicing law on the side. He made enough money to go to Chicago and get his start. The joke-loving, rugged individualists of eastern Tennessee threw open the doors of hospitality and embraced him with friendship.

The on-the-scene defense personnel prepared for battle. Some of the scientific witnesses and advisers had arrived, and Arthur Garfield Hays had come down from New York.

Once in Dayton, Hays remained until the conclusion of the trial. In all the accounts of the trial I have read, Hays is mentioned but is not given credit for the important role he played. Darrow, and Darrow alone, had charge of developing the testimony of the defense witnesses; but if there was a master mind developing the overall strategy of the defense, it was Hays. Every time I was present, he acted as moderator of the small group of legal strategists. If he proposed or endorsed a plan, it became an integral part of the defense procedure. The few times he actively entered into the court proceedings, he demonstrated that he could hold his own on the level of the refined and cultured, but if the fight called for it he could sling mud with the best of mudslingers. His sympathy, understanding, and the fight he waged for justice were genuine.

We had promised the A.C.L.U. in New York that we would continue the fight for federal jurisdiction. On the date of our hearing,

Darrow, Hays, Neal, and I drove to Cookville. The judge called our case at 11 :00 A.M. The attorneys filed the necessary papers and gave the oral arguments. At ten minutes of twelve we had concluded the presentation of our side.

The news releases simply stated that the federal judge had denied our plea, but there is a little more to the story. We expected a decision not earlier than Monday or Tuesday of the following week. That would have given the judge time to study—or pretend he had studied —the transcript of the oral argument. But we were caught off base. The judge rendered his decision to deny us a change of venue by reading a *prepared* statement, probably written the day he gave us a place on his calendar. By five minutes to twelve, we were looking for a place to get lunch. To me, it seemed that the decision was based upon bias and not upon a study of our legal position.

In any case, if we had been granted a change of venue, Colby might have replaced Darrow and Darrow would have lost this last chance to meet Bryan in a public debate. I believe now that Darrow was trying to conceal it, but he was more than pleased with the federal judge's decision. Furthermore, the A.C.L.U. at New York seemed to be satisfied that we had done all that we could. All efforts now could be directed toward the trial which definitely would take place in Dayton.

The trial opened following my being reindicted (the first indictment had been hastily and improperly drawn up). The first three days were largely given to selecting a jury and to presenting the defense's motion to quash the indictment. Darrow's speech in which he argued that the anti-evolution law violated the principles of freedom guaranteed by the constitution of the state of Tennessee was a noteworthy opening volley.[1]

The arguments regarding the constitutionality of the law were ended at the recess of a morning session. William K. Hutchinson, INS reporter whom I had gotten to know well, was waiting for me on the courthouse steps. He wanted to take me to lunch, but he first wanted to overtake Judge John T. Raulston who was already half a block down the street. We soon overtook the Judge. Hutchinson started a conversation during which he slipped in a few compliments and flattering remarks about the Judge—how smoothly and efficiently he was running the court, how impartial he was, and what extensive

1 See p. 41.

legal knowledge he was displaying. Two questions, if I remember correctly, were then innocently addressed to the Judge: "Are you going to render your decision on the constitutionality of the law when court convenes this afternoon?" "That is my intention," answered Judge Raulston with dignity. "Will the admissibility of the scientific testimony be the next order of business?" "That is my understanding," replied the Judge, not realizing that he had just made his decision public. In short, the Judge had decided to deny the motion to quash the indictment: the trial would proceed.

I thought Hutchinson was going to expose the trap he had set by running away too quickly. It had been so easy that Hutchinson was afraid some other reporter would come along and try the same thing, in which case he would of course have lost his scoop. We finally got away from the Judge so that Hutchinson could get his story to the main office of the INS. I am sure that what happened in the court that afternoon and the following morning has been reported in detail many times but in widely varying accounts. The Judge, completely enthralled with himself and the importance of his job, probably would not have realized what he had done, but he was prodded into action by a reporter who discovered that he had been scooped by an unknown colleague.

After reading the morning papers the next day, Judge Raulston appointed an investigating committee to learn the identity and motives of an "unknown reporter." The following day the committee made its report in the midst of the solemnly assembled court. "We find that the information came from the Court." The Judge uttered a single word, "Well!" Nevertheless, after collecting himself, he called Hutchinson before the bench for a brief lecture on the proper behavior of reporters toward judges.

The conflict between Darrow and Bryan is famous, but Bryan and Malone also faced one another angrily at least on one occasion. It took place at one of the afternoon sessions in the courtroom proper, before the Judge moved proceedings to the courthouse lawn under the shade trees. Bryan and Malone monopolized this particular session. The technical point that was being argued was forgotten and was not, to my knowledge, mentioned after the first five minutes of Bryan's speech.[2] Bryan addressed the Judge, then immediately turned to face the spectators. There was no pretense; this was to be a

2 See pp. 47–48.

speech to the people, not merely to the court. It was a general defense
of his position in his fight for the cause of fundamentalism. I did not
pay much attention to the text of the speech, but it was well received
by the audience. I remember being lulled into a feeling that I cannot
accurately describe. Since I was not listening to what he was saying,
but to how he was saying it, I was letting his oratorical talents
hypnotize me. Every gesture and intonation of his voice blended
so perfectly that it was almost like a symphony; and yet, the impression was that it was all extemperaneous. The longer he talked
(a little more than an hour), the more complete was the control he
had over the crowd. As I listened I thought Bryan must have sensed
victory as he moved toward the climax of his speech. Indeed, it
looked as if he had sparked a force and enthusiasm that might lead to
victory for fundamentalism in a number of states of the Union. I
thought to myself that if something were not done—and done in a
hurry—the forces of enlightenment were in for a severe battle. Bryan
received a long and spirited—but not boisterous—ovation. No attempt was made seriously to bring order in the court. A few
faces in the audience were blank and expressionless; all others showed
reverence and worship.

For many in the courtroom, however, Malone's reply was unex-
pectedly moving. He was not an oratorical wizard like Bryan, but
those talents which he possessed, he knew how to use effectively. He
was a great dramatic actor, a master at playing upon the emotions
and at communicating bitter sarcasm and ridicule behind a screen
of pretended sympathy and understanding which produced interest
and later endorsement of his actual viewpoint. His answer to Bryan
combined with a rapid presentation of the defense case took only
twenty-five minutes. But in that brief time, the people were eating
out of his hand and had, for the time being, forgotten Bryan.

At the conclusion of the speech bedlam broke loose in the form of
loud applause. An Irish policeman from Chattanooga was acting
bailiff of the court. He was using his night stick to pound on a table
near ours. Another officer who had been stationed among the
spectators rushed to the bailiff and offered to help restore order.
The Irishman replied, "I'm not trying to restore order. Hell, I'm
cheering." That night stick must have been spiked with a generous
shot of lead, for he split the table top in half and sent splinters of
wood flying all over that section of the courtroom. The Judge knew
that order could not be restored; accordingly he adjourned the court

and ordered the room cleared. After some time and much difficulty, the room was cleared.

Bryan, Malone, and I were the only ones that remained. Bryan, seated in his comfortable chair, had his legs stretched out and was staring at a spot on the floor two or three feet beyond his feet. Malone was partially seated on the defense attorney's table intently looking at Bryan. I was at the table waiting for one or the other to make the first move. Bryan heaved a big sigh and looked up at Malone. In a subdued, slightly quivering voice, he said, "Dudley, that was the greatest speech I have ever heard." Malone, who had served as Undersecretary of State during Bryan's appointment as Secretary of State under Woodrow Wilson, spoke quietly to his old chief, "Thank you, Mr. Bryan; I am terribly sorry that I was the one that had to do it." It all seemed so plain to me; I thought anyone could have seen what was transpiring. Bryan was crushed.

But after a night's rest he was revitalized; his instinct to fight, his courage, and his strong heart would not let him completely surrender. All of his actions and everything he said throughout the remainder of the trial were efforts to mend the damage, reestablish himself with the public, and, above all, regain his old spirit and self-confidence.

As to events that took place on the afternoon of the famous examination of Bryan by Darrow, the transcript clearly outlines what happened, but does not include all that occurred. A court reporter cannot record what two people are saying at the same time, much less what six or seven screaming individuals are saying simultaneously. As soon as Bryan was called to be the defense's expert witness on the Bible, the Judge, Tom Stewart, the Hickses, and the other members of the prosecution team present were waving their arms and shouting objections. Bryan was up and talking but, unlike the others, he was trying to restore order. It was obvious that the Judge did not intend to permit Bryan to take the stand; when Bryan had restored order, however, he pleaded to be allowed to testify.

The people sitting out in the courtroom still considered him their leader. They considered the Bryan-Malone tilt as one round of the fight. Bryan had been knocked down, but he would win in the end. One might think that Bryan had had enough experience in political chicanery to see that it was a mistake to take the stand, but he was fighting himself. He had to have a personal victory and he believed that he was more than a match for Darrow on the subject of the

Bible. The transcript tells the story of this encounter—the most dramatic event of the trial. Bryan tried to stage a comeback, but Darrow blocked him completely. This time, the people who heard and saw the event lost their confidence in Bryan; he would never regain the confidence of many of them.

On the eighth day of the trial, I was convicted of the crime of teaching the Darwinian concept of evolution, for which I was fined $100.[3] H. L. Mencken, acting in behalf of the Baltimore *Evening Sun,* either paid or guaranteed the payment of my fine. I could now go any place I wished without violating the law; and being free for a few days I went to Lexington, Kentucky, to visit some of my former professors.

I do not remember now why, but I was due to be in Dayton on Monday of the following week. On Sunday I was on my way back to Tennessee. Somewhere along the way I ran into Paul Y. Anderson of the St. Louis *Post-Dispatch* and learned about Mr. Bryan's death. Paul had been told at a ticket office that in order to get to Dayton, he would have to go through Chattanooga, arriving in Dayton the next morning at nine o'clock. This was quite unsatisfactory, and he asked if I knew of any way to get to Dayton by five o'clock that afternoon. I said that I did—if he had the price of a taxi fare. He obtained a refund for me on my ticket, purchased two more for Athens and we were on our way. In Athens we took a taxi to Dayton.

In going from Athens to Dayton, the traveler crosses the Tennessee River by means of a ferry at a hamlet called Washington. The ferry happened to be on the west side of the river when we arrived; consequently we were in a good location for observing who came across from the Dayton side. Judge Raulston was one of the passengers, and as he passed us he nodded but the nod was so slight we did not recognize it as a greeting. The driver said, "You know who that was? That was Judge Raulston who was the Judge in that 'Monkey Trial.' I wish I was in his place; I would have seen that Scopes, Darrow and all the rest of those d—— atheists got tarred and feathered and railed out of the State." He talked the rest of the way to Dayton. I found out, in no uncertain words, what some people thought of my colleagues and me. Paul got out at the hotel and the driver took me to the Bailey residence where I roomed. I leaned

3 This fine imposed by Judge Raulston would cause the Tennessee Supreme
   Court in January, 1927, to reverse the lower court's verdict on a technicality
   —in Tennessee, fines in excess of $50 must be fixed by a jury.

against the car with my head in the window opposite the driver: "I want to thank you for a very pleasant trip. It was more than a pleasure because it helps me maintain my confidence in humanity when I encounter a fellow who has positive convictions and is not afraid to stand up for those convictions. I would consider it an honor if you would give me your name and permit me to introduce myself. My name is John Scopes." If I had not moved quickly, I might have been killed, he made his getaway so fast.

The next day some of my friends from Washington, Tennessee, were in town. They said the driver had stopped in front of the post office after returning to Washington and said in an excited voice to a group of loafers, "I've had those s.o.b.'s, Scopes and Darrow, in my car all afternoon and did not know it!" Darrow, I am sure, would have considered it a compliment.

I had wanted to get back as soon as possible to express my sympathy to the Bryan family and offer my services; but by the time I arrived there, so many people were trying to be of assistance that I would have only added to the confusion. The most Christian thing I could do was to keep out of the way and hope that Mrs. Bryan would learn from others of my sympathy for her and her family.

In a few days, I had finished my business, packed my belongings, and left Dayton to spend the rest of the summer with my family in Paducah. I fully intended to be a regular visitor to Dayton since that year had been one of the most pleasant years of my life. I had met many people I liked and wanted to continue to call friends. But the realities of a career alter the course for many of us. I have been able to visit Dayton only twice in forty years.

I cannot help wondering what would have been the outcome of the whole issue if we could have gotten our case into the federal courts. To be sure everyone connected with the defense was positive that the U.S. Supreme Court, before whom we hoped the case would ultimately go, would render a decision in favor of the defense. How could the court do otherwise when the law infringed on academic freedom and the freedom of speech? Those two infringements on our liberties were grounds enough to condemn the law.

I am sure that the Supreme Court, as it was then constituted, would have recognized a second violation of our personal liberties, for the Butler Act was an effort on the part of a religious group, the fundamentalists, to impose by law their religious beliefs on the rest of society.

Our Founding Fathers, acquainted with the bloody religious wars in Europe, had written into the Constitution the right of religious freedom and had further provided, by means of the doctrine of the separation of church and state, that no religious group should control or unduly influence any arm of secular government. I believe that had we reached the Supreme Court we would have been victorious on this issue.

We did not, in fact, get to the federal courts. What, then, did we actually accomplish?

The defense had hoped to call a number of scientists as witnesses. They were to testify in regard to the erroneous belief that there was an irreconcilable conflict between the theory of evolution and the Genesis account. One scientist made it to the stand, but Judge Raulston shortly ruled that scientific testimony was not admissible. I think that was a defeat for us, but only in the terms of our legal goals. The material sent out from Dayton through the news media included the interviews and the affidavits of the scientific witnesses; these made a tremendous impact on the science education of the country and the world.

A second accomplishment was the limiting of the passing of anti-evolution bills in other states. This was achieved through the activities of six groups of people: the defense team and their aids who organized and presented our case; scientists; theologians; educators who worked then and are continuing to work for a better concept of education and the freedom of inquiry; the large numbers of ordinary citizens who thought or were capable of learning to think by the simple process of reasoning from cause to effect; and last, but by no means least, the news media. The efforts of these groups, I think, were responsible for limiting the passing of anti-evolution bills to only two additional states, Mississippi and Arkansas.

The trial created a better climate for understanding divergent points of view. The intermingling of a great number of people from all over our country (where did they find accommodations?) and the news gathered and sent out by reporters from the North, East, South, and West lowered to some extent the barriers of misunderstanding that separated the different sections of our country. By no means were these barriers demolished but the top rails were removed or splintered.

The trial marked a beginning of the development of a national consciousness of the roles played by religion, science, and education.

I think the importance of communicating the thinking of the professionals in these fields to the general public was first generally appreciated during and immediately after the trial.

I believe that the Dayton trial marked the beginning of the decline of fundamentalism. Each year—as the result of someone's efforts to better interpret what the defense was trying to do—more and more people are reached. This, in conjunction with the labor of scientists, educators, ministers and with the dissemination of the results of their efforts through books and news media, has retarded the spread of fundamentalism.

But most importantly, I feel that restrictive legislation on academic freedom is forever a thing of the past, that religion and science may now address one another in an atmosphere of mutual respect and of a common quest for truth. I like to think that the Dayton trial had some part in bringing to birth this new era.

I have had a continuing interest in the issues of the trial but never as a participant. Many times I have been asked why I have had no further role to play relative to the issues—even why I did not at least capitalize on my publicity and reap the monetary harvest that was close at hand. Perhaps my best answer is to paraphrase Calvin Coolidge's "I do not choose to run"; for me it would be, "I did not choose to do so."

John T. Scopes with his father Thomas Scopes in July, 1925.

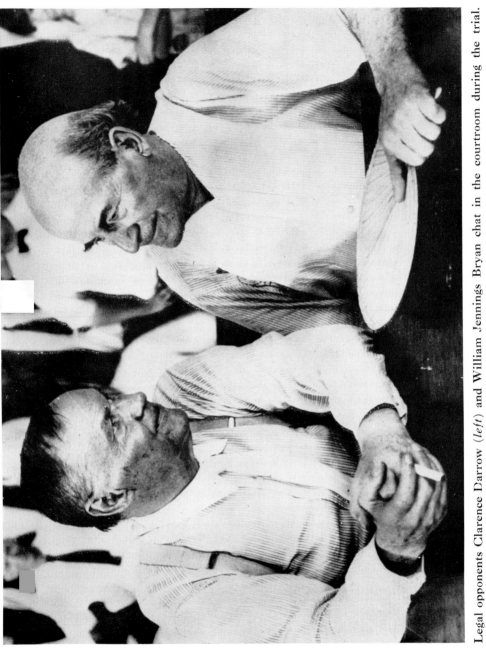

Legal opponents Clarence Darrow (*left*) and William Jennings Bryan chat in the courtroom during the trial.

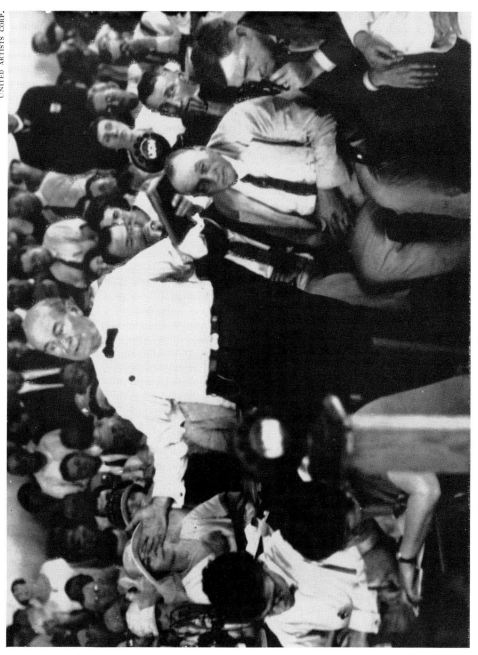

Prosecutor Bryan addresses the court during the Dayton trial.

The gentlemen of the jury, July, 1925.

Some of the scientists and lawyers who rallied to the defense. (*Left to right, front row*) Wilbur Nelson, Fay-Cooper Cole, W. C. Curtis, unidentified, J. G. Lipman; (*middle row*) J. R. Neal, M. M. Metcalf, Charles Potter, W. L. McCloskey, William A. Kepner, Arthur Garfield Hays, H. Wheelock; (*back row*) E. Haldeman-Julius, George W. Rappleyea, Frank Thone, and Watson Davis.

H. L. Mencken, iconoclastic reporter for the Baltimore *Evening Sun.*

John T. Scopes and the granddaughter of William Jennings Bryan, Helen Rudd Owen Brown, before the witness stand in the courtroom where Scopes stood trial thirty-five years before.

John T. Scopes views the marker which the Tennessee Historical Commission has erected on the courthouse grounds at Dayton.

PART TWO

THE TRIAL

DARROW: *Mr. Bryan, do you believe that the first woman was Eve?*

BRYAN: *Yes.*

DARROW: *Do you believe that she was literally made out of Adam's rib?*

BRYAN: *I do.*

DARROW: *Did you ever discover where Cain got his wife?*

BRYAN: *No sir; I leave the agnostics to hunt for her.*

Transcript of the trial
July 20, 1925

"THE MONKEY TRIAL":
A Reporter's Account

H. L. MENCKEN

HENRY LOUIS MENCKEN, a protagonist on the American literary scene of the 1920's, studied engineering at Baltimore Polytechnic Institute before turning to a literary career in 1899. His caustic criticism of American culture evoked cries of both delight and anguish from his readers. Revealing the iconoclast at work, the excerpts which follow (from his dispatches of July 9–18, 1925, to the Baltimore *Evening Sun*) are reprinted here for the first time.[1]

July 9 (the day preceding the opening of the trial)

On the eve of the great contest Dayton is full of sickening surges and tremors of doubt. Five or six weeks ago, when the infidel Scopes was first laid by the heels, there was no uncertainty in all this smiling valley. The town boomers leaped to the assault as one man. Here was an unexampled, almost a miraculous chance to get Dayton upon the front pages, to make it talked about, to put it upon the map. But how now?

Today, with the curtain barely rung up and the worst buffooneries to come, it is obvious to even town boomers that getting upon the map, like patriotism, is not enough. The getting there must be managed discreetly, adroitly, with careful regard to psychological niceties. The boomers of Dayton, alas, had no skill at such things,

---

1 These excerpts are used by permission of the Mercantile-Safe Deposit and Trust Company, Baltimore, Maryland, the executor of Mr. Mencken's literary estate, and by permission of the Baltimore *Evening Sun.*

and the experts they called in were all quacks. The result now turns
the communal liver to water. Two months ago the town was obscure
and happy. Today it is a universal joke.

I have been attending the permanent town meeting that goes on
in Robinson's drug store, trying to find out what the town optimists
have saved from the wreck. All I can find is a sort of mystical confidence that God will somehow come to the rescue to reward His old
and faithful partisans as they deserve—that good will flow eventually
out of what now seems to be heavily evil. More specifically, it is
believed that settlers will be attracted to the town as to some refuge
from the atheism of the great urban Sodoms and Gomorrahs.

But will these refugees bring any money with them? Will they buy
lots and build houses? Will they light the fires of the cold and silent
blast furnace down the railroad tracks? On these points, I regret to
report, optimism has to call in theology to aid it. Prayer can accomplish a lot. It can cure diabetes, find lost pocketbooks and re-
strain husbands from beating their wives. But is prayer made any
more efficacious by giving a circus first? Coming to this thought,
Dayton begins to sweat.

The town, I confess, greatly surprised me. I expected to find a
squalid Southern village, with darkies snoozing on the horseblocks,
pigs rooting under the houses and the inhabitants full of hookworm
and malaria. What I found was a country town full of charm and even
beauty—a somewhat smallish but nevertheless very attractive Westminster or Belair.

The houses are surrounded by pretty gardens, with cool green
lawns and stately trees. The two chief streets are paved from curb to
curb. The stores carry good stocks and have a metropolitan air,
especially the drug, book, magazine, sporting goods and soda-water
emporium of the estimable Robinson. A few of the town ancients
still affect galluses and string ties, but the younger bucks are very
nattily turned out. Scopes himself, even in his shirt sleeves, would
fit into any college campus in America save that of Harvard alone.

Nor is there any evidence in the town of that poisonous spirit which
usually shows itself when Christian men gather to defend the great
doctrine of their faith. I have heard absolutely no whisper that
Scopes is in the pay of the Jesuits, or that the whisky trust is backing
him, or that he is egged on by the Jews who manufacture lascivious
moving pictures. On the contrary, the Evolutionists and the Anti-

Evolutionists seem to be on the best of terms and it is hard in a group to distinguish one from the other.

The basic issues of the case, indeed, seem to be very little discussed at Dayton. What interests everyone is its mere strategy. By what device, precisely, will Bryan trim old Clarence Darrow? Will he do it gently and with every delicacy of forensics, or will he wade in in high gear and make a swift butchery of it? For no one here seems to doubt that Bryan will win—that is, if the bout goes to a finish. What worries the town is the fear that some diabolical higher power will intervene on Darrow's side—that is, before Bryan heaves him through the ropes. . . .

July 10 (the first day)

The trial of the infidel Scopes, beginning here this hot, lovely morning, will greatly resemble, I suspect, the trial of a prohibition agent accused of mayhem in Union Hill, N. J. That is to say, it will be conducted with the most austere regard for the highest principles of jurisprudence. Judge and jury will go to extreme lengths to assure the prisoner the last and least of his rights. He will be protected in his person and feelings by the full military and naval power of the State of Tennessee. No one will be permitted to pull his nose, to pray publicly for his condemnation or even to make a face at him. But all the same he will be bumped off inevitably when the time comes, and to the applause of all right-thinking men.

The real trial, in truth, will not begin until Scopes is convicted and ordered to the hulks. Then the prisoner will be the Legislature of Tennessee, and the jury will be that great, fair, unimpassioned body of enlightened men which has already decided that a horse hair put into a bottle will turn into a snake and that the Kaiser started the late war. What goes on here is simply a sort of preliminary hearing, with music by the village choir. For it will be no more possible in this Christian valley to get a jury unprejudiced against Scopes than it would be possible in Wall Street to get a jury unprejudiced against a Bolshevik.

I speak of prejudice in its purely philosophical sense. As I wrote yesterday, there is an almost complete absence in these pious hills of the ordinary and familiar malignancy of Christian men. If the Rev. Dr. Crabbe ever spoke of bootleggers as humanely and affectionately as the town theologians speak of Scopes, and even Darrow and Malone, his employers would pelt him with their spyglasses and sit on him until the ambulance came from Mount Hope. There is absolutely no bitterness on tap. But neither is there any doubt. It has been decided by acclamation, with only a few infidels dissenting, that the hypothesis of evolution is profane, inhumane and against God, and all that remains is to translate that almost unanimous decision into the jargon of the law and so have done.

The town boomers have banqueted Darrow as well as Bryan, but there is no mistaking which of the two has the crowd, which means the venire of tried and true men. Bryan has been oozing around the country since his first day here, addressing this organization and that, presenting the indubitable Word of God in his caressing, ingratiating way, and so making unanimity doubly unanimous. From the defense yesterday came hints that he was making hay before the sun had legally begun to shine—even that it was a sort of contempt of court. But no Daytonian believes anything of the sort. What Bryan says doesn't seem to these congenial Baptists and Methodists to be argument; it seems to be a mere graceful statement of the obvious. . . .

July 11

To call a man a doubter in these parts is equal to accusing him of cannibalism. Even the infidel Scopes himself is not charged with any such infamy. What they say of him, at worst, is that he permitted himself to be used as a cat's-paw by scoundrels eager to destroy the anti-evolution law for their own dark and hellish ends. There is, it appears, a conspiracy of scientists afoot. Their purpose is to break down religion, propagate immorality, and so reduce mankind to the level of the brutes. They are the sworn and sinister agents of Beelzebub, who yearns to conquer the world, and has his eye especially upon Tennessee. Scopes is thus an agent of Beelzebub once removed, but that is as far as any fair man goes in condemning him. He is young and yet full of folly. When the secular arm has done execution upon him, the pastors will tackle him and he will be saved.

The selection of a jury to try him, which went on all yesterday afternoon in the atmosphere of a blast furnace, showed to what extreme lengths the salvation of the local primates has been pushed. It was obvious after a few rounds that the jury would be unanimously hot for Genesis. The most that Mr. Darrow could hope for was to sneak in a few men bold enough to declare publicly that they would have to hear the evidence against Scopes before condemning him.

The slightest sign of anything further brought forth a peremptory challenge from the State. Once a man was challenged without examination for simply admitting that he did not belong formally to any church. Another time a panel man who confessed that he was prejudiced against evolution got a hearty round of applause from the crowd.

The whole process quickly took on an air of strange unreality, at least to a stranger from heathen parts. The desire of the judge to be fair to the defense, and even polite and helpful, was obvious enough—in fact, he more than once stretched the local rules of procedure in order to give Darrow a hand. But it was equally obvious that the whole thing was resolving itself into the trial of a man by his sworn enemies. A local pastor led off with a prayer calling on God to put down heresy; the judge himself charged the grand jury to protect the schools against subversive ideas. And when the candidates for the petit jury came up Darrow had to pass fundamentalist after fundamentalist into the box—some of them glaring at him as if they expected him to go off with a sulphurous bang every time he mopped his bald head.

In brief this is a strictly Christian community, and such is its notion of fairness, justice and due process of law. Try to picture a town made up wholly of Dr. Crabbes and Dr. Kellys, and you will have a reasonably accurate image of it. Its people are simply unable to imagine a man who rejects the literal authority of the Bible. The most they can conjure up, straining until they are red in the face, is a man who is in error about the meaning of this or that text. Thus one accused of heresy among them is like one accused of boiling his grandmother to make soap in Maryland. He must resign himself to being tried by a jury wholly innocent of any suspicion of the crime he is charged with and unanimously convinced that it is infamous. Such a jury, in the legal sense, may be fair. That is, it may be willing to hear the evidence against him before bumping him off. But it would certainly be spitting into the eye of reason to call it impartial.

The trial, indeed, takes on, for all its legal forms, something of the air of a religious orgy. The applause of the crowd I have already mentioned. Judge Raulston rapped it down and threatened to clear the room if it were repeated, but he was quite unable to still its echoes under his very windows. The courthouse is surrounded by a large lawn, and it is peppered day and night with evangelists. One and

all they are fundamentalists and their yells and bawlings fill the air
with orthodoxy. . . .

July 13 (the second day)

There is a Unitarian clergyman here from New York, trying
desperately to horn into the trial and execution of the infidel Scopes.
He will fail. If Darrow ventured to put him on the stand the whole
audience, led by the jury, would leap out of the courthouse windows,
and take to the hills. Darrow himself, indeed, is as much as they
can bear. The whisper that he is an atheist has been stilled by the
bucolic make-up and by the public report that he has the gift of
prophecy and can reconcile Genesis and evolution. Even so, there is
ample space about him when he navigates the streets. The other day
a newspaper woman was warned by her landlady to keep out of the
courtroom when he was on his legs. All the local sorcerers predict
that a bolt from heaven will fetch him in the end. The night he
arrived there was a violent storm, the town water turned brown, and
horned cattle in the lowlands were afloat for hours. A woman back in
the mountains gave birth to a child with hair four inches long,
curiously bobbed in scallops.

Dr. Kelly should come down here and see his dreams made real.
He will find a people who not only accept the Bible as an infallible
handbook of history, geology, biology and celestial physics, but who
also practice its moral precepts—at all events, up to the limit of
human capacity. It would be hard to imagine a more moral town
than Dayton. If it has any bootleggers, no visitor has heard of them.
Ten minutes after I arrived a leading citizen offered me a drink made
up half of white mule and half of coca cola, but he seems to have
been simply indulging himself in a naughty gesture. No fancy
woman has been seen in the town since the end of the McKinley
administration. There is no gambling. There is no place to dance. The
relatively wicked, when they would indulge themselves, go to
Robinson's drug store and debate theology.

In a word, the new Jerusalem, the ideal of all soul savers and sin
exterminators. Nine churches are scarcely enough for the 1,800
inhabitants; many of them go into the hills to shout and roll. A
clergyman has the rank and authority of a major-general of artillery.
A Sunday-school superintendent is believed to have the gift of
prophecy. But what of life here? Is it more agreeable than in Baby-
lon? I regret that I must have to report that it is not. The incessant

clashing of theologians grows monotonous in a day and intolerable the day following. One longs for a merry laugh, a burst of happy music, the gurgle of a decent jug. Try a meal in the hotel; it is tasteless and swims in grease. Go to the drug store and call for refreshment; the boy will hand you almost automatically a beaker of coca cola. Look at the magazine counter: a pile of *Saturday Evening Posts* two feet high. Examine the books: melodrama and cheap amour. Talk to a town magnifico: he knows nothing that is not in Genesis.

I propose that Dr. Kelly be sent here for sixty days, preferably in the heat of summer. He will return to Baltimore yelling for a carboy of pilsner and eager to master the saxophone. His soul perhaps will be lost, but he will be a merry and a happy man.

[On the second day of the trial Darrow spoke at length on upholding a law which makes it a crime to teach a certain scientific theory. His closing remarks follow.]

If today you can take a thing like evolution and make it a crime to teach it in the public schools, tomorrow you can make it a crime to teach it in the private schools, and the next year you can make it a crime to teach it in the hustings or in the churches. At the next session you may ban it in books and in newspapers. Soon you may set Catholic against Protestant and Protestant against Protestant, and try to foist your own religion upon the minds of men. . . . After a while, your Honor, it is the setting of man against man and creed against creed until with flying banners and beating drums we are marching backward to the glorious ages of the sixteenth century when bigots lighted fagots to burn the men who dared to bring any intelligence and enlightenment and culture to the human mind.

July 14 (the third day)

The net effect of Clarence Darrow's great speech yesterday seems to be precisely the same as if he had bawled it up a rainspout in the interior of Afghanistan. That is, locally, upon the process against the infidel Scopes, upon the so-called minds of these fundamentalists of upland Tennessee. You have but a dim notion of it who have only read it. It was not designed for reading, but for hearing. The clangtint of it was as important as the logic. It rose like a wind and ended like a flourish of bugles. The very judge on the bench, toward the end of it, began to look uneasy. But the morons in the audience, when it was over, simply hissed it.

During the whole time of its delivery the old mountebank, Bryan, sat tight-lipped and unmoved. There is, of course, no reason why it should have shaken him. He has these hill billies locked up in his pen and he knows it. His brand is on them. He is at home among them. Since his earliest days, indeed, his chief strength has been among the folk of remote hills and forlorn and lonely farms. Now with his political aspirations all gone to pot, he turns to them for religious consolations. They understand his peculiar imbecilities. His nonsense is their ideal of sense. When he deluges them with his theological bilge they rejoice like pilgrims disporting in the river Jordan.

Darrow's peroration yesterday was interrupted by Judge Raulston, but the force of it got into the air nevertheless. This year it is a misdemeanor for a country school teacher to flout the archaic nonsense of Genesis. Next year it will be a felony. The year after the net will be spread wider. Pedagogues, after all, are small game; there are larger birds to snare—larger and juicier. Bryan has his fishy eye on them. He will fetch them if his mind lasts, and the lamp holds out to burn. No man with a mouth like that ever lets go. Nor ever lacks followers. . . .

July 15 (the fourth day)

The cops have come up from Chattanooga to help save Dayton from the devil. Darrow, Malone and Hays, of course, are immune to constabulary process, despite their obscene attack upon prayer. But all other atheists and anarchists now have public notice they must shut up forthwith and stay shut so long as they pollute this bright, shining, buckle of the Bible belt with their presence. Only one avowed infidel has ventured to make a public address. The Chattanooga police nabbed him instantly, and he is now under surveillance in a hotel. Let him but drop one of his impious tracts from his window and he will be transferred to the town hoose-gow. . . .

A preacher of any sect that admits the literal authenticity of Genesis is free to gather a crowd at any time and talk all he wants. More, he may engage in a disputation with any other expert. I have heard at least a hundred such discussions, and some of them have been very acrimonious. But the instant a speaker utters a word against divine revelation he begins to disturb the peace and is liable to immediate arrest and confinement in the calaboose beside the railroad tracks.

Such is criminal law in Rhea county as interpreted by the uniformed and freely sweating agents. As I have said, there are high legal authorities in Chattanooga who dissent sharply, and even argue that the cops are a set of numbskulls and ought to be locked up as public nuisances. But one need not live a long, incandescent week in the Bible belt to know that jurisprudence becomes a new science as one crosses the border. Here the ordinary statutes are reinforced by Holy Writ, and whenever there is a conflict Holy Writ takes precedence.

Judge Raulston himself has decided, in effect, that in a trial for heresy it is perfectly fair and proper to begin proceedings with a prayer for the confutation and salvation of the defendant. . . .

Rhea county is very hospitable and, judged by Bible belt standards, very tolerant. The Dayton Babbitts gave a banquet to Darrow, despite the danger from lightning, meteors and earthquakes. Even Malone is treated politely, though the very horned cattle in the fields know that he is a Catholic and in constant communication with the Pope. But liberty is one thing and license is quite another. Within the bounds of Genesis the utmost play of opinion is permitted and even encouraged. An evangelist with a new scheme for getting into Heaven can get a crowd in two minutes. But once a speaker admits a doubt, however cautiously, he is handed over to one of the secular arm.

Two Unitarian clergymen are prowling around the town looking for a chance to discharge their "hellish heresies." . . . Yesterday afternoon a Jewish rabbi from Nashville also showed up. Marks by name. He offered to read and expound Genesis in Hebrew, but found no takers. The Holy Rollers hereabout, when they are seized by the gift of tongues, avoid Hebrew, apparently as a result of Ku Klux influence. Their favorite among all the sacred dialects is Hittite. It sounds to the infidel like a series of college yells.

Judge Raulston's decision yesterday afternoon in the matter of Hays' motion was a masterpiece of unconscious humor. The press stand, in fact, thought he was trying to be jocose deliberately and let off a guffaw that might have gone far if the roar of applause had not choked it off. Hays presented a petition in the name of the two Unitarians, the rabbi and several other theological "reds," praying that in selecting clergymen to open the court with prayer hereafter he choose fundamentalists and anti-fundamentalists alternately. The petition was couched in terms that greatly shocked and enraged the prosecution. When the judge announced that he would leave nomination of the chaplain to the Pastors' Association of the town there was the gust of mirth aforesaid, followed by howls of approval. The

Pastors' Association of Dayton is composed of fundamentalists so powerfully orthodox that beside them such a fellow as Dr. John Roach Straton [2] would seem an Ingersoll. . . .

The witnesses of the defense, all of them heretics, began to reach town yesterday and are all quartered at what is called the Mansion, an ancient and empty house outside the town limits, now crudely furnished with iron cots, spittoons, playing cards and the other camp equipment of scientists. Few, if any, of these witnesses will ever get a chance to outrage the jury with their blasphemies, but they are of much interest to the townspeople. The common belief is that they will be blown up with one mighty blast when the verdict of the twelve men, tried and true, is brought in, and Darrow, Malone, Hays and Neal with them. The country people avoid the Mansion. It is foolish to take unnecessary chances. Going into the courtroom with Darrow standing there shamelessly and openly challenging the wrath of God, is risk enough.

The case promises to drag into next week. The prosecution is fighting desperately and taking every advantage of its superior knowledge of the quirks of local procedure. The defense is heating up and there are few exchanges of courtroom amenities. There will be a lot of oratory before it is all over and some loud and raucous bawling otherwise, and maybe more than one challenge to step outside. The cards seem to be stacked against poor Scopes, but there may be a joker in the pack. Four of the jurymen, as everyone knows, are Methodists and a Methodist down here belongs to the extreme wing of liberals. Beyond him lie only the justly and incurably damned. . . .

July 16 (the fifth day)

Two things ought to be understood clearly by heathen Northerners who follow the great cause of the State of Tennessee against the infidel Scopes. One is that the old mountebank, Bryan, is no longer thought of as a mere politician and jobseeker in these Godly regions, but has become converted into a great sacerdotal figure, half man and half archangel—in brief, a sort of fundamentalist pope. The other is that the fundamentalist mind, running in a single rut for fifty years,

2 Dr. John Roach Straton, Baptist minister and active member of the Anti-Saloon League of America, was a prolific writer and frequent lecturer at this time. His many books included *Salvation of Society: Menace of Immorality in Church and State* (1920), and *Our Relapse Into Paganism* (1921).

is now quite unable to comprehend dissent from its basic superstitions, or to grant any common honesty, or even any decency, to those who reject them. . . .

In view of the fact that everyone here looks for the jury to bring in a verdict of guilty, it might be expected that the prosecution would show a considerable amiability and allow the defense a rather free play. Instead, it is contesting every point very vigorously and taking every advantage of its greatly superior familiarity with local procedure. There is, in fact, a considerable heat in the trial. Bryan and the local lawyers for the State sit glaring at the defense all day and even the Attorney-General, A. T. Stewart, who is supposed to have secret doubts about fundamentalism, has shown such pugnacity that it has already brought him to forced apologies.

The high point of yesterday's proceedings was reached with the appearance of Dr. Maynard M. Metcalf of the Johns Hopkins.[3] The doctor is a somewhat chubby man of bland mien, and during the first part of his testimony, with the jury present, the prosecution apparently viewed him with great equanimity. But the instant he was asked a question bearing directly upon the case at bar there was a flurry in the Bryan pen and Stewart was on his feet with protests. Another question followed, with more and hotter protests. The judge then excluded the jury and the show began.

What ensued was, on the surface, a harmless enough dialogue between Dr. Metcalf and Darrow, but underneath there was very tense drama. At the first question Bryan came out from behind the State's table and planted himself directly in front of Dr. Metcalf, and not ten feet away. The two McKenzies followed, with young Sue Hicks at their heels.

Then began one of the clearest, most succinct and withal most eloquent presentations of the case for the evolutionists that I have ever heard. The doctor was never at a loss for a word, and his ideas flowed freely and smoothly. Darrow steered him magnificently. A word or two and he was howling down the wind. Another and he hauled up to discharge a broadside. There was no cocksureness in him. Instead he was rather cautious and deprecatory and sometimes he halted and confessed his ignorance. But what he got over before

3 An eminent zoologist who wrote extensively within his chosen field, Dr. Metcalf had also been a Bible teacher in the Congregational church at one time.

he finished was a superb counterblast to the fundamentalist buncombe. The jury, at least, in theory heard nothing of it, but it went whooping into the radio and it went banging into the face of Bryan.

Bryan sat silent through the whole scene, his gaze fixed immovably on the witness. Now and then his face darkened and his eyes flashed, but he never uttered a sound. It was, to him, a string of blasphemies out of the devil's mass—a dreadful series of assaults upon the only true religion. The old gladiator faced his real enemy at last. Here was a sworn agent and attorney of the science he hates and fears—a well-fed, well-mannered spokesman of the knowledge he abominates. Somehow he reminded me pathetically of the old Holy Roller I heard last week—the mountain pastor who damned education as a mocking and a corruption. Bryan, too, is afraid of it, for wherever it spreads his trade begins to fall off, and wherever it flourishes he is only a poor clown.

But not to these fundamentalists of the hills. Not to the yokels he now turns to for consolation in his old age, with the scars of defeat and disaster all over him. To these simple folk, as I have said, he is a prophet of the imperial line—a lineal successor to Moses and Abraham. The barbaric cosmogony that he believes in seems as reasonable to them as it does to him. They share his peasant-like suspicion of all book learning that a plow hand cannot grasp. They believe with him that men who know too much should be seized by the secular arm and put down by force. They dream as he does of a world unanimously sure of Heaven and unanimously idiotic on this earth.

This old buzzard, having failed to raise the mob against its rulers, now prepares to raise it against its teachers. He can never be the peasants' President, but there is still a chance to be the peasants' Pope. He leads a new crusade, his bald head glistening, his face streaming with sweat, his chest heaving beneath his rumpled alpaca coat. One somehow pities him, despite his so palpable imbecilities. It is a tragedy, indeed, to begin life as a hero and to end it as a buffoon. But let no one, laughing at him, underestimate the magic that lies in his black, malignant eye, his frayed but still eloquent voice. He can shake and inflame these poor ignoramuses as no other man among us can shake and inflame them, and he is desperately eager to order the charge.

In Tennessee he is drilling his army. The big battles, he believes, will be fought elsewhere.

July 17 (the sixth day)

Though the court decided against him this morning, and the testimony of the experts summoned for the defense will be barred out of the trial of the infidel Scopes, it was Dudley Field Malone who won yesterday's great battle of rhetoricians. When he got upon his legs it was the universal assumption in the courtroom that Judge Raulston's mind was already made up, and that nothing that any lawyer for the defense could say would shake him. But Malone unquestionably shook him. He was, at the end, in plain doubt, and he showed it by his questions. It took a night's repose to restore him to normalcy. The prosecution won, but it came within an inch of losing.

Malone was put up to follow and dispose of Bryan, and he achieved the business magnificently. I doubt that any louder speech has ever been heard in a court of law since the days of Gog and Magog. It roared out of the open windows like the sound of artillery practice, and alarmed the moonshiners and catamounts on distant peaks. Trains thundering by on the nearby railroad sounded faint and far away and when, toward the end, a table covered with standing and gaping journalists gave way with a crash, the noise seemed, by contrast, to be no more than a pizzicato chord upon a viola da gamba. The yokels outside stuffed their Bibles into the loud-speaker horns and yielded themselves joyously to the impact of the original. In brief, Malone was in good voice. It was a great day for Ireland. And for the defense. For Malone not only out-yelled Bryan, he also plainly out-generaled and out-argued him. His speech, indeed, was one of the best presentations of the case against the fundamentalist rubbish that I have ever heard.

It was simple in structure, it was clear in reasoning, and at its high points it was overwhelmingly eloquent. It was not long, but it covered the whole ground and it let off many a gaudy skyrocket, and so it conquered even the fundamentalists. At its end they gave it a tremendous cheer—a cheer at least four times as hearty as that given to Bryan. For these rustics delight in speechifying, and know when it is good. The devil's logic cannot fetch them, but they are not above taking a voluptuous pleasure in his lascivious phrases.

The whole speech was addressed to Bryan, and he sat through it in his usual posture, with his palm-leaf fan flapping energetically and his hard, cruel mouth shut tight. The old boy grows more and more pathetic. He has aged greatly during the past few years and begins to look elderly and enfeebled. All that remains of his old fire is now in his black eyes. They glitter like dark gems, and in their glitter there is immense and yet futile malignancy. That is all that is left of the Peerless Leader of thirty years ago. Once he had one leg in the White House and the nation trembled under his roars. Now he is a tinpot pope in the coca-cola belt and a brother to the forlorn pastors who belabor half-wits in galvanized iron tabernacles behind the railroad yards. His own speech was a grotesque performance and downright touching in its imbecility. Its climax came when he launched into a furious denunciation of the doctrine that man is a mammal. It seemed a sheer impossibility that any literate man should stand up in public and discharge any such nonsense. Yet the poor old fellow did it. Darrow stared incredulous, Malone sat with his mouth wide open, Hays indulged himself one of his sardonic chuckles. Stewart and Bryan *fils* looked extremely uneasy, but the old mountebank ranted on. To call a man mammal, it appeared, was to flout the revelation of God. The certain effect of the doctrine would be to destroy morality and promote infidelity. The defense let it pass. The lily needed no gilding.

There followed some ranting about the Leopold-Loeb case, culminating in the argument that learning was corrupting—that the colleges by setting science above Genesis were turning their students into murderers. Bryan alleged that Darrow had admitted the fact in his closing speech at the Leopold-Loeb trial, and stopped to search for the passage in a printed copy of the speech. Darrow denied making any such statement, and presently began reading what he actually had said on the subject. Bryan then proceeded to denounce Nietzsche, whom he described as an admirer and follower of Darwin. Darrow challenged the fact and offered to expound what Nietzsche really taught. Bryan waved him off.

The effect of the whole harangue was extremely depressing. It quickly ceased to be an argument addressed to the court—Bryan, in fact, constantly said "My friends" instead of "Your Honor"—and became a sermon at the camp meeting. All the familiar contentions of the Dayton divines appeared in it—that learning is dangerous, that nothing is true that is not in the Bible, that a yokel who goes to church regularly knows more than any scientist ever heard of. The thing went to fantastic lengths. It became a farrago of puerilities without coherence or sense. I don't think the old man did himself justice. He was in poor voice and his mind seemed to wander. There was far too much hatred in him for him to be persuasive. . . .

These Tennessee mountaineers are not more stupid than the city proletariat; they are only less informed. If Darrow, Malone and Hays could make a month's stumping tour in Rhea county, I believe that fully a fourth of the population would repudiate fundamentalism, and that not a few of the clergy now in practice would be restored to their old jobs on the railroad. Malone's speech yesterday probably shook a great many true believers; another like it would fetch more than one of them. But the chances are heavily against them ever hearing a second. Once this trial is over, the darkness will close in again, and it will take long years of diligent and thankless effort to dispel it—if, indeed, it is ever dispelled at all. . . .

I described Stewart the other day as a man of apparent education and sense and palpably superior to the village lawyers who sit with him at the trial table. I still believe that I described him accurately. Yet even Stewart toward the close of yesterday's session gave an exhibition that would be almost unimaginable in the North. He began his reply to Malone with an intelligent and forceful legal argument, with plenty of evidence of hard study in it. But presently he slid into a violent theological harangue, full of extravagant nonsense. He described the case as a combat between light and darkness and almost descended to the depths of Bryan. Hays challenged him with a question. Didn't he admit, after all, that the defense had a tolerable case; that it ought to be given a chance to present its evidence? I transcribe his reply literally:

"That which strikes at the very foundations of Christianity is not entitled to a chance."

Hays, plainly astounded by this bald statement of the fundamentalist view of due process, pressed the point. Assuming that the defense would present, not opinion but only unadorned fact, would Stewart still "object to its admission"? He replied,

"Personally, yes."

"But as a lawyer and Attorney-General?" insisted Hays.

"As a lawyer and Attorney-General," said Stewart, "I am the same man."

Such is justice where Genesis is the first and greatest of law books and heresy is still a crime.

July 18

All that remains of the great cause of the State of Tennessee against the infidel Scopes is the formal business of bumping off the defendant.

There may be some legal jousting on Monday and some gaudy oratory on Tuesday, but the main battle is over, with Genesis completely triumphant. Judge Raulston finished the benign business yesterday morning by leaping with soft judicial hosannas into the arms of the prosecution. The sole commentary of the sardonic Darrow consisted of bringing down a metaphorical custard pie upon the occiput of the learned jurist.

"I hope," said the latter nervously, "that counsel intends no reflection upon this court."

Darrow hunched his shoulders and looked out of the window dreamily.

"Your honor," he said, "is, of course, entitled to hope."

No doubt the case will be long and fondly remembered by connoisseurs of judicial delicatessen—that is, as the performances of Weber and Fields are remembered by students of dramatic science. In immediate restrospect, it grows more fantastic and exhilerating. Scopes has had precisely the same fair trial that the Hon. John Philip Hill,[4] accused of bootlegging on the oath of Howard A. Kelly,[5] would have before the Rev. Dr. George W. Crabbe. He is a fellow not without humor; I find him full of smiles today. On some near tomorrow the Sheriff will collect a month's wages from him, but he has certainly had a lot of fun. . . .

The Scopes trial, from the start, has been carried on in a manner exactly fitted to the anti-evolution law and the simian imbecility under it. There hasn't been the slightest pretense to decorum. The rustic judge, a candidate for re-election, has postured before the yokels like a clown in a ten-cent side show, and almost every word he has uttered has been an undisguised appeal to their prejudices and superstitions. The chief prosecuting attorney, beginning like a competent lawyer and a man of self-respect, ended like a convert at a Billy Sunday revival. It fell to him, finally, to make a clear and astounding statement of theory of justice prevailing under fundamentalism. What he said, in brief, was that a man accused of infidelity had no rights whatever under Tennessee law. . . .

Darrow has lost this case. It was lost long before he came to

4 The Honorable John Philip Hill, recipient of a silver star during World War I, was at this time serving as Congressman from Maryland.
5 Dr. Howard A. Kelly was at this time a consultant in gynecology at Johns Hopkins; highly respected in his field and a prolific writer, he was an eminent Baltimore resident.

Dayton. But it seems to me that he has nevertheless performed a great public service by fighting it to a finish and in a perfectly serious way. Let no one mistake it for comedy, farcical though it may be in all its details. It serves notice on the country that Neanderthal man is organizing in these forlorn backwaters of the land, led by a fanatic, rid of sense and devoid of conscience. Tennessee, challenging him too timorously and too late, now sees its courts converted into camp meetings and its Bill of Rights made a mock of by its sworn officers of the law. There are other States that had better look to their arsenals before the Hun is at their gates.

[Except for an editorial written after his return to Baltimore, this was the last Mencken dispatch on the trial.]

PART THREE

ACADEMIC FREEDOM

Your Honor, I feel that I have been convicted of violating an unjust statute. I will continue in the future, as I have in the past, to oppose this law in any way I can. Any other action would be in violation of my ideal of academic freedom—that is, to teach the truth as guaranteed in our constitution of personal and religious freedom. I think the fine is unjust.

JOHN THOMAS SCOPES
July 21, 1925

DAYTON'S FIRST ISSUE

ROGER N. BALDWIN

R OGER N. BALDWIN, born in 1884, received his A.B. and
A.M. degrees from Harvard. He taught sociology at Washington University, St. Louis, before becoming director of the American Civil Liberties Union in 1917. Serving in that post until 1950, he meanwhile acted as an adviser to the U.N., as a consultant on civil liberties for the U.S. occupation forces in Japan and Korea, and in a similar capacity in Germany and Austria. Although he was not present at Dayton in 1925, he and his staff at the A.C.L.U. laid the strategy for the Scopes trial.

As one of the few living actors in that forty-year-old drama—the only trial in American history for teaching evolution in a public school —I may fairly claim a special warrant for drawing on both memory and record to recount the events. I add to them evidence of the continuing conflict today between religious bigotry and scientific teaching, drawn from replies to circular inquiries sent to state departments of education in the South and Southwest and to the publishers of biology textbooks.

The trial of John Thomas Scopes originated in the office of the American Civil Liberties Union in New York; I was then serving as its director. The A.C.L.U. had been formed only five years previously by citizens concerned about the many violations of the Bill of Rights, for the purpose of rendering free legal aid in the courts to any persons with a claim deserving action. We took note of reports of violations in the press, offering to the defendants the services of our numerous volunteer lawyers, located throughout the country.

When we read press reports of what seemed to us a fantastic proposal pending in the Tennessee legislature to make the teaching of evolution a crime, we kept an eye on it, incredulous that it would become law. When the governor signed the bill we at once prepared a press release for the Tennessee papers, offering to defend any teacher prosecuted under it. That was the origin of probably the most widely reported trial on a public issue ever to have taken place in the United States. It was further dramatized by the two contending chief counsels, William Jennings Bryan, on behalf of the World's Christian Fundamentals Association, for a literal belief in Genesis, and Clarence Darrow, agnostic, for the defense of science.

Even before these two protagonists entered the case, the indictment of Scopes had been startling enough by itself to arouse the press to sense a great news story. We in the A.C.L.U. were not aware of the magnitude of the issue that we had raised by our offer in the Tennessee papers to defend any teacher violating the law. We had accepted almost as a routine response the telephoned proposal from a businessman in Dayton, Tennessee, George W. Rappleyea, who offered as a willing challenger, a young high school biology teacher, John Thomas Scopes. We subsequently confirmed our offer of legal aid and told Scopes to present himself to the prosecutor and await indictment.

Back of that event lay more history than we knew. We had only read press dispatches reporting that the Tennessee legislature was debating such a law for the first time in any state. We did not know that it had its origin in the fundamentalist fervor of a first-term farmer-legislator (J. Washington Butler), who had been inspired by hearing William Jennings Bryan lecture on the Good Book. Bryan had several years before secured a resolution by the Florida legislature condemning the teaching of evolution, without criminal penalty, and he counseled Tennessee to do the same. But Butler wanted penalties, and he persuaded the legislature to go along. The Tennessee House adopted his bill 71 to 5 (January 21, 1925), and the Senate obligingly followed with a vote of 24 to 6. How could legislators, faced with the issue, vote against God and the Bible and for monkeys? That was the question. The few opponents protested, feeling confident, as one of them stated, that the governor would veto the bill. But he signed, observing that "probably the law will never be applied." It was then, in the spring of 1925, that the papers carried the news and the A.C.L.U. promptly made its offer.

The law appeared to conflict with two provisions of the Tennessee constitution which were not even mentioned in the legislative debates, one to the effect that "no preference shall ever be given to any religious establishment," and the other an injunction "to cherish literature and science." The constitution also denied public office to "disbelievers in God or immortality," but that point was not raised against Scopes. (The U.S. Supreme Court has since voided such a requirement for public office.)

While we in the A.C.L.U. were beset by journalists demanding stories about whom the lawyers would be, what defense we would put up, and when we expected to go to trial, we were unable to answer. Our directors were divided. Should we enlist conservative constitutional lawyers and make it a top issue of separation of church and state, freedom of teaching the truth as laid down by the very textbook which Scopes taught, approved by the state? Or should we make it a contest between religion and the unreasonable restraint on science imposed by law? Should we attempt to get into the federal courts with an injunction against enforcing a state law violative of the First Amendment guarantees?

We were advised by different lawyers on quite contrary courses. The issue was novel; it was dramatic. On advice of a distinguished lawyer a feeble move was made to appeal to the federal courts but it was dropped before submission. While we were debating among ourselves the type of defense we should pursue, the decision was made for us by the sudden offer of William Jennings Bryan to appear as counsel assisting the attorney general of Tennessee. It was immediately apparent what kind of a trial it would be: the Good Book against Darwin, bigotry against science, or, as popularly put, God against monkeys. With Bryan for the prosecution, it was almost inevitable that Clarence Darrow should volunteer for the defense. Darrow was well known as an agnostic; he frequently wrote and lectured on the subject, ridiculing many of the Old Testament myths. Some of our more constitutional-minded lawyers, foreseeing what kind of a trial it would be, demurred. But Darrow's offer was accepted with enthusiasm by the one man qualified to determine it, Scopes himself. Darrow was aided both by Tennessee lawyers who volunteered their services and by well-known attorneys for the A.C.L.U., Arthur Garfield Hays, later its general counsel, and Dudley Field Malone, a liberal Democratic politician who had been Collector of the Port of New York.

But between the lineup of counsel in April and the next scheduled session of the grand jury in August, there was to be an intolerable wait for us and for the avid newspapermen. Consequently the presiding circuit judge in Dayton was persuaded to call a special grand jury in May which promptly returned the desired indictment, and the judge (John Raulston) set the trial for July 10.

The story of that trial is too well known from play and movie to be repeated. A published volume reports it word for word, including the highly publicized and devastating examination by Darrow of Bryan as an expert witness on the Bible, later expunged by the judge from the official record as improperly admitted.

The lawyers, of course, made the usual motions to quash the indictment on the ground that the law was unconstitutional for indefiniteness, for establishing a religion, for unreasonableness, and for destroying freedom of thought and speech. Scopes pleaded not guilty on the ground that the law was unconstitutional, although he admitted teaching the banned subject. But his defense was a matter of law, not fact, so he never testified. The students he taught, however, testified to what he so readily admitted teaching.

The trial, lasting ten days in the Rhea County courthouse, turned on the clash of the two protagonists Bryan and Darrow. The legal issues faded into obscurity against the vivid advocacies of an unquestioning faith and of a rational and probing common sense. Bryan threw his challenge to the defense lawyers, stating, "These gentlemen . . . did not come here to try this case. They came here to try revealed religion. I am here to defend it. . . . I am simply trying to protect the Word of God against the greatest athiest or agnostic in the United States." And Darrow replied to him, "We have the purpose of preventing bigots and ignoramuses from controlling the education of the United States and you know it, and that is all." [1]

The defense was prepared to call an array of expert witnesses, scientists and others, to testify to the theory of evolution, but the judge would not allow any expert testimony on the ground that it was irrelevant to the charge. The law was specific on what could not be taught and no amount of testimony as to its truth would mitigate the crime. Thus the hopes of the defense to enlighten public opinion were

1 Quotes are from the official transcript of the trial, seventh day, page 743.

thwarted. The prosecution, too, was thwarted in its plans to call expert rebuttal witnesses on biblical truth.

The judge charged the jury that what had been admitted was sufficient for conviction, that Scopes had taught that man was descended, in theory at least—and theory constituted the offense—from a lower order of animals. Something was made of the point that Scopes had not taught that doctrine "instead" of the Bible story of creation, as the law required, but the judge ruled it out. It was enough to have taught it. The jury took only nine minutes to reach the expected verdict. Scopes was fined $100, the minimum penalty fixed by the act. Notice of appeal to the state supreme court was filed and Scopes, the unheard offender, left the state to take up the offer of a scholarship for advanced studies.

With an appeal in prospect on constitutional points, we in the A.C.L.U. were urged from several influential sources to engage a different type of counsel. Darrow, Hays, and Malone might be first-rate for such a performance as that required with Bryan as the chief prosecutor, but the supreme court of Tennessee was no place for a contest of wits and philosophies of religion and science. It was not to be an easy case in law. The state had the undoubted power to prescribe the curriculum for public schools. Had it the power to do so unreasonably by outlawing a particular theory? Had it the power to establish a religion, the biblical story of creation, and to deny a contrary theory? It was conceded that the law could abolish all teaching of biology, but that it could not impose a false one; but what was false and who was to judge? Were there federal questions, and if so, what? The U.S. Supreme Court had not then, as now, applied to the states the First Amendment rights, and it was doubtful even if the Court would review such a case. Congress could make no law establishing a religion, but could a state?

With these difficult options, other lawyers were brought in, among them Walter Pollack of New York, a constitutional authority; Samuel Rosensohn, a conservative in his interpretation of the law; and two Tennessee lawyers, one a law school dean, who served along with Hays and Darrow. The lawyers filed with the state supreme court a lengthy brief of 141 pages, covering all possible arguments, but stressing most strongly, because they believed it gave the court a more acceptable ground for reversal, the indefiniteness of the statute. What did it mean to "teach," or to teach "instead," and what exactly was the meaning of "descent"? Although the brief emphasized the conflict of the law with the Tennessee constitutional provision against giving "preference to any religious establishment," no great hope was entertained that the court would regard Genesis as a religious establishment.

The appeal was argued before the court on June 1, 1926, a year after the trial, by Clarence Darrow and his Tennessee associates. Six months later, in January, 1927, the court rendered its decision. Of the five judges, one did not take part; he was new on the bench. Of the other four, two upheld the law as a proper exercise of the police power of the state to control education, and another went along reluctantly with them holding, however, in a concurring opinion, that only "materialistic theories of evolution" were barred and that "if God played some role in it, it could be taught." The fifth dissented. The majority held that the law had "a relation to a legitimate object within the State power and is not to be condemned as arbitrary or capricious."

In sustaining the law the court reversed the conviction on the technical ground that the fine had been imposed by the judge, not the jury, as the law provided. The real reason, of course, was to prevent an appeal to the U.S. Supreme Court. But the court had a poor view of the whole case, instructing the attorney general not to reinstate it and adding, "We see nothing to be gained by prolonging the life of this bizarre case."

Thus the most-publicized trial in American history on the complex issue of church and state, freedom of teaching, religion versus science, came to its legal end. Some lawyers proposed pushing it further in the federal courts by various collateral attacks on the law, but they were discouraged by the prospect of poor results. Years later, when the Supreme Court had extended federal jurisdiction to protect individual rights from invasion by the states, the same principles urged by the defense in the Dayton trial outlawed school prayers, Bible-reading, and all other religious intrusions into public education.

If forty years after the 1925 evolution trial in Dayton, Tennessee, the issue seems academic history, suitable only for the drama of a stage play and a movie, we reckon without the persistence of the opponents of science determined to uphold the biblical story of creation. Never yielding their opposition, they have in half a dozen states renewed their attacks on biology textbooks which teach evolution as a theory. The upsurge of pressure is evidently part of the crusade of the extreme political right where fundamentalists find a congenial home.

The laws penalizing persons convicted of teaching the theory of evolution remain on the books of three states: Tennessee, Arkansas, and Mississippi. Although nobody has since been prosecuted for the heresy, school boards and teachers are cautious. The caution extends far beyond these three states. In one, the state board of education attempted to ward off criticism by inserting in all biology textbooks, inside the front cover where it cannot be missed, the warning that "its official position is that the theory of evolution should be presented as theory only and not as fact." In another southern state the commissioner of education reports that "since there is tremendous feeling regarding the teaching of evolution in the public schools, and since there is so much else of great importance to teach besides the theory of evolution, it is the part of wisdom to avoid the topic just as much as possible."

These boards of education need not worry. Even the textbooks approved by the American Institute of Biological Science do not go so far as to assert evolution of man as a fact. The evidence for the evolution of the lower orders may be presented convincingly enough, but for man himself, not yet. With this dubious escape from a collision with Genesis, school boards and textbook commissions have been able to prevail against their fundamentalist critics in those areas, mainly the South and Southwest, where the controversy has again broken out in recent years.

The issue has only been slumbering all this time. Textbook publishers, queried on their policies, report a timidity in treating evolution up to a few years ago when the American Institute of Biological Science adopted several approved textbooks and thus gave authority and courage to hesitant boards. One publisher writes, "We have long been aware that references to the theory of evolution can jeopardize the adoption of a text-book series in several parts of the country." Another writes, "Authors and publishers have long been very much aware that, with certain people and certain groups and in certain areas of the country, the treatment of evolution in high school biology text-books and general science text-books is scrutinized with special care. In the past a few publishers have reacted by minimizing or disguising the topic, or, in some cases, omitting it entirely. In recent years, following the appearance of the Biological Sciences Curriculum Study text-books, evolution has become less controversial. Even so, the text-books make it clear that evolution is still a theory."

Another publisher, more aware of politics, writes of the revived attack under the growth of the extreme right wing in American politics: "There is seemingly an increasing amount of pressure which is attempting to equate any reference to any type of evolution with atheism, and this pressure is often associated with the use of the word, 'Communism.' "

The confusion of terms is deliberate. Right-wing propaganda against "atheistic communism" identifies evolution as one of communism's materialistic tenets. In 1964, a preacher in Arizona, promoting a referendum petition for a popular vote on evolution, described it in terms that removed it from science into the sectarian doctrine of atheism, and therefore called for it to be prohibited in public schools. His referendum petition failed for want of sufficient signatures.

But it is clear that the fundamentalist drive still has sufficient vitality to renew a controversy that seemed to have been settled years ago. It was not settled by the Tennessee courts, which sustained the law, but by the many years of public ridicule of any attempt to establish Genesis as the official explanation of the origins of the universe and any attempt to punish any teacher in public schools who taught the contrary. Yet ridicule did not prevent a brief and local drive for law to enthrone Genesis when, in 1925 and 1927, Mississippi adopted an anti-evolution law and Arkansas followed with one adopted by a popular vote of almost two to one after the Arkansas state legislature had refused to be stampeded into action. They were gestures to the Faith. Nobody was again prosecuted, although the teaching of evolution was generally taboo in the states which had banned it. The laws remain in force with no specific decision on their constitutionality.

In view of the later decisions of the U.S. Supreme Court outlawing prayers and Bible-reading in public schools, there seems no doubt that an anti-evolution law establishing Genesis as scientific and religious dogma would be held void. But it is most unlikely that the courts will get a challenge. No prosecutor would be so ill-advised as to act against a teacher in the three states with laws. A test case might be brought—and in one state it has been threatened—to enjoin the use of particular biology textbooks on the ground that their treatment of evolution violates the free exercise of religion clause of the Constitution by denying what Bible literalists teach.

But the contention is too far-fetched to be entertained; no religion is denied by teaching a theory or even a fact. Genesis is not denied or attacked; it is simply ignored like any other religious explanation of creation. What the fundamentalists never understand is that the United States is not legally a Christian country, that all religions are equal and that the government may show no preferences.

Equally untenable is the contention advanced by some fundamentalists that the teaching of evolution establishes a religion, atheism, on the ground that both belief and disbelief in God as the creator is "religious." But such advocates read themselves out of court by their own contention, for if disbelief is barred so is belief.

The controversy over teaching evolution may be with us for a long time to come but the likelihood of its ever getting into the courts is remote. It has been a long way from that summer in Dayton to the present-day ruling of the Supreme Court, which bans the intrusion of any religion into the public schools. Educators and textbook publishers alike know where they stand.

The age-old conflict between bigotry and enlightenment, freedom and dogma, is not over, but Dayton was a great historic guidepost on the road to emancipation in the search for truth.

PART FOUR

THE SCIENTISTS

After all whether Mr. Bryan knows it or not, he is a mammal, he is an animal and he is a man. . . . There is never a duel with the truth. The truth always wins and we are not afraid of it. We are ready to tell the truth as we understand it, and we do not fear all the truth that they can present as facts.

DUDLEY FIELD MALONE
July 16, 1925

THE MEN OF SCIENCE

WATSON DAVIS

W ATSON DAVIS earned his B.S. degree in engineering from George Washington University. He has been director and editor of Science Service, a nonprofit institution for the popularization of science, since 1933. For nearly thirty years, he conducted a CBS radio program on which he interviewed over a thousand scientists. In addition to being a member of the Science Service team at the Dayton trial, he was active in aiding the defense to secure the testimonies of various science experts throughout the country.

To the public, which was informed largely through the daily press in those early radio days, the 1925 Scopes trial in Dayton, Tennessee, was a dramatic confrontation between the silver-tongued orator William Jennings Bryan and the great trial lawyer and liberal Clarence Darrow. It was a clash of personalities occasioned by an artificially engendered legal trial. While it lacked the risk and drama of a human life in balance that a murder trial has, the threat to human liberties and freedom of education was so great that it became the public event most widely covered by the press up to its time.

Freedom of education and freedom of science were in a very real sense in peril. And those of scientific and liberal mind and inclination took this opportunity to explain to the public, through the press, the great issue of liberty of thought as well as validity of scientific fact and implication. Like the debate between Thomas Henry Huxley and

Bishop Samuel Wilberforce at the 1860 meeting of the British Association for the Advancement of Science, following Charles Darwin's publication of *Origin of Species,* the Scopes trial provided a jousting field between "revealed religion" and the growing body of scientific research which showed that human beings are a part of the organic evolution of life.

At the time the Dayton situation developed, Science Service, the Institution for the Popularization of Science, was four years old. It had been created in 1921 through the joint efforts of scientists and newspaper men. Science Service was sustained by the financing of E. W. Scripps, the founder of Scripps-Howard newspapers, and scientifically and intellectually stimulated by William E. Ritter, biologist of the University of California.

The purpose of Science Service was to take science to the public through the press. Coverage of science by newspapers was then in its infancy and hardly respectable in most editorial offices of the daily press. It was even more disdained in many research laboratories and universities. Science Service, since its formation, had been urging the newspapers to consider science as serious, important news. We did this not merely by arguing theoretically that science was important and should be covered in the same way that politics, sports, and drama are, but by utilizing those who were skilled in both science and newspaper writing to prepare a daily report. As a consequence, the news and feature material on science was good copy and was published by newspapers to which it was distributed on a nonprofit basis.

When the situation in Dayton developed in which the Bible seemed to be pitted against science, it was quite appropriate for Science Service to have its writers in the press corps covering the event. We went further by offering aid in the defense of John T. Scopes, and the legal talent marshaled by the American Civil Liberties Union welcomed this aid.

About a month before the trial began, I took a trip to the Pacific Coast on a news-gathering visit to science institutions and universities. In those days, the trip to the west coast from the east was not a few hours by air, but a relatively long and arduous train trip of not less than four or five days, making it necessary to be away from one's office for approximately one month to make it worthwhile.

On the way, I stopped at Dayton to look over the situation and make hotel reservations for the coming trial. (The date for the trial was set well in advance with the cooperation of the Tennessee courts and the enthusiastic promotional aid of the business and general community efforts of the Dayton, Tennessee, region.) I took this opportunity to tramp through some of the hills surrounding the valley in which the little town of Dayton lies and to look at the geology. With the help of geologic maps, I wrote a few stories which contended that the hills around Dayton in the record of the rocks testified to the validity of evolution. These features as well as other preliminary releases were distributed to the newspapers in our service. These releases were either written by or were interviews with the leading scientists of the time who explained the background of evolution in considerable detail.

On our staff at the time of the trial was Frank Thone, Ph.D. in ecology, who wrote expertly on biology and related subjects. He and I were the Science Service team that traveled to Dayton to report the trial. Daily stories by Thone and myself were wired to over a score of newspapers which were Science Service clients. The first director of Science Service was Dr. Edwin E. Slosson; while he did not go to Dayton he gave enthusiastic support to the Dayton trial coverage.

On the way to Dayton, Arthur Garfield Hays and Dudley Field Malone traveled from New York to Tennessee by train, passing through Washington, where Dr. Thone and I joined them. We immediately began planning the scientific phases of the defense. During the trip Thone and I suggested those scientists who might be asked to come to Dayton and testify as to the facts of evolution—experts in geology, zoology, anthropology, psychology, and sociology. We felt strongly that those to be invited should be eminent, authoritative, and able to express themselves well. We did not hope to enlist those whose positions at that time were so demanding that they could not spare the couple of weeks necessary for continued attendance at the trial— for instance, Henry Fairfield Osborn, the great paleontologist and anthropologist, then head of the American Museum of Natural History, or David Starr Jordan, perhaps the leading biologist of the day. We did suggest those experts who actually came: Dr. Fay-Cooper Cole, Dr. W. C. Curtis, Professor William Kepner, Professor Jacob G. Lipman, Professor Kirtley F. Mather, Professor Maynard M. Metcalf, Professor Wilbur A. Nelson, and Professor Horatio H. Newman.

As the train moved westward through Virginia and Tennessee,

telegrams were dispatched by Hays and Malone on behalf of the American Civil Liberties Union. The response was enthusiastic. So many of the scientists, potential witnesses for the defense, assembled at Dayton that it was necessary for Rappleyea, general manager of the operation on behalf of Scopes, to rehabilitate a large unused residence on the mining company property for housing them and the legal staff.

When Dr. Thone and I moved to these defense headquarters, The Mansion, I relinquished the room reservations that I had made some weeks before in the principal hotel of Dayton. My reservations were picked up very promptly by a Unitarian minister, who unfortunately contracted typhoid and died of the disease not long after the trial ended. How many other typhoid cases there were under the crowded conditions in Dayton those days, I do not know, but I imagine that one of the reasons that many of us did not contract typhoid was that we had the immunization which was given in connection with army service prior to and during World War I.

Dr. Thone and I arrived in Dayton about three days before the beginning of the trial. The attitude of the townfolk and the people from the surrounding region was not too cordial to the invaders from the North, for the "yokels" felt that these "foreigners" were attacking the Bible and the true religion.

From the hills there came the backwoods-dwellers who had been listening to fundamentalist revivalists and other preachers for some weeks prior to the trial. They had been told of the danger to religious belief from the invasion of "foreigners," scientists, lawyers, and those who would do damage to the Bible and its holy word. Some of these "hillbillies" came into town with squirrel rifles over their shoulders. I thought this was rather ominous, but the defense lawyers—Darrow, Malone, and Hays—seemed to rather enjoy the prospect of this kind of conflict.

Bryan had already arrived in town, and he, of course, was the champion of the religionists, but the three defense lawyers, with their characteristic interest in people, went into the streets and talked to the people there. Soon the rifles disappeared; the neighborhood evidently had decided that there could be two sides to this controversy after all and that this trial should be worth listening to. They decided to sit back and see what would happen.

After all, the jury was to be selected from the people of the neighborhood, and it was good tactics for the defense lawyers to get acquainted with the kind of people who would be on the jury. Actually, the jury had nothing to do except to form a backdrop for the legal pyrotechnics during the trial.

The author of the Tennessee evolution law who had introduced the bill in the legislature was shown a Catholic Bible which the defense had brought for possible use at the trial. While he was obviously very much on Bryan's side of the case, he admitted that he had never known that there was more than one kind of Bible. I imagine the only Bible known in that region of Tennessee before this time was the King James version.

By the time the actual trial opened there was, thanks to the perception of the townspeople and their observations of the defense lawyers, the feeling that this was not a cut-and-dried case and that people from outside Tennessee were not necessarily all devils. In the good American tradition, a trial was justified.

The defense effort from the standpoint of scientific evidence concentrated upon biological and geological science. Sociology, human behavior, and comparative religion were not emphasized. H. L. Mencken, the literary "sage of Baltimore" who was at the trial representing the Baltimore *Evening Sun,* with his insight into human nature and his sharp and inquisitive mind was the closest approach to a social scientist on the scene. Mencken and I occupied the same table in the courtroom not more than a dozen feet away from the judge's bench. We did some extra-curricular observation of local religion and reported it. I remember one Sunday we obtained relief from court, which was not in session on the Sabbath, by going to observe a Holy Roller baptism in a nearby creek. I borrowed, from Dr. Thone, the idea that this was a "relict endemic." The readers can work this out for themselves, but baptism in this sense was a sort of survival of primitive religion. The idea may not have been pleasing to the participants but I doubt if they ever heard about it.

The scientific information that was prepared at defense headquarters was not allowed in the court testimony. But the press carried the planned testimony to the public. The largest array of telegraph press facilities used up to that time was established in Dayton. Dozens of key instruments together with old-fashioned telegraphers sent many thousands of words a day during the course of the trial.

The material issued at Dayton, along with the commentary of scientists who, though not at the trial, were interviewed by newspapermen, made an impact upon the public. It served to give information which otherwise would not have been distributed to the press. The drama of two great legal lights contending upon a highly emotional matter, the validity of the Bible as a scientific document, and the fundamental religious emotions prevalent in those days provided a vehicle of great educational importance.

Perhaps I am overlooking the question of the fundamental principles of freedom of thought and liberty of religion and understanding which was implicit in the whole trial. It was civil liberty, liberty of the mind that was at stake, as it is still in many parts of the world.

When the motion picture *Inherit the Wind* was produced as a fictionalized documentary of the Scopes trial, I returned to Dayton for the world premiere on the thirty-fifth anniversary of the trial (July 21, 1960). Of the hundreds of newspaper men who were there in 1925 only a few could be located. The contending legal lights, Bryan and Darrow included, were long since dead. The judge and practically all the jury had disappeared. John T. Scopes, now retired, modest and unassuming as always, was the central figure at the revisitation.

Radio, in its toddling stage at the time of the 1925 trial, was used as a scientific wonder to broadcast from the courtroom; today it is a common thing, even in Dayton, which has its own local station. Listening to the radio, in my comfortable motel room in the town's outskirts, I realized that the morning programs were revivalist in tone as a result of the alarm experienced by the new generation of fundamentalists at the renewed anti-Bible propaganda which they conceived the motion picture to be. Scopes and a few other pro-evolutionists, including myself, were invited to broadcast as an "equal-time" gesture.

Before making this revisitation, I had optimistically written, "The law is a dead letter but still on the statute books." But my reportorial foray to Dayton resulted in my retracting my earlier optimism about evolution and Tennessee and subsequently I wrote:

Anti-evolution is far from dead in Tennessee.

It is usual to hear good citizens say that the law is a dead letter and unenforced. It is true that teachers are not being arrested and brought to trial, not even in a test case as John T. Scopes was in the case in which Bryan and Darrow were legal adversaries.

Nevertheless, the prohibition against teaching evolution is effective, far more effective than prohibition of alcoholic beverages stronger than beer. The mere possession of hard liquor is illegal but no one with the price goes thirsty.

No teacher who wants to hold his job teaches evolution. There are too many fundamentalist preachers ready to attack any foolhardy professor to risk trouble in that way. It would be far safer to take an illegal drink. The vocal pro-evolutionist would not be hauled into court, but he probably would find his job insecure, his contract unrenewed or the climate uncongenial.

Unlike alcohol, there is no prohibition on students drinking at the font of scientific wisdom, quaffing great gulps of Darwinism, even during school hours, if the forbidden knowledge sufficiently intrigues them. The good ministers who believe literally in the Genesis account of creation (who believe, as one of them proclaimed, the Bible cover to cover and the covers as well!) may intimidate and close the minds of some students with their constant harangues, but the students are at least free to read what they will.

A professor of the University of Tennessee who was in Dayton during the celebration told me that the book that he used in a biology course had a chapter on evolution. When he came to that chapter in the book he told his students that this could not be taught under the Tennessee law. He was convinced that all of the students read the chapter, perhaps even more assiduously than if it had been assigned and explained in class.

The biological unity of life is a scientific fact that extends far beyond the conflict between the biblical account of Genesis and the findings of science. The process of convincingly informing the people of scientific truth is laborious and unending. Dramatic events like the Scopes trial are part of the continuous renaissance of scientific understanding.

THE EVOLUTION CONTROVERSY

W. C. CURTIS

W INTERTON C. CURTIS, born in 1875, received his Ph.D. from Johns Hopkins University in 1901 and began teaching zoology that same year at the University of Missouri. His entire academic career was spent there, culminating with his becoming Professor Emeritus of Zoology and Dean Emeritus of the College of Arts and Science of the university in 1946. One of the scientists invited to testify for the defense in the Scopes trial, he was never permitted to take the stand.

In September, 1901, when I began my teaching at the University of Missouri, the evidence for evolution and its causal factors was one of the topics that ran through my course in General Zoology and one that was brought together in review and summary toward the end of the course as standard procedure in such teaching. A few years later I began offering a course, entitled Theory of Evolution, which was continued until my retirement in 1946.

In my teaching I made it a point not to discuss the religious involvements, except as necessary in contrasting the doctrine of special creation with that of evolution and the impact of the evolutionary concept in other fields. In class I made no attempt to proselyte but let the facts speak for themselves in favor of evolution as the historic course of events in the story of life. If a student wanted to talk with me "man-to-man" outside class, I was available and felt free to express my convictions with respect to the conflict between religious beliefs and the doctrine of evolution. Many were the discussions I had in the lecture room after class, in my office, or in my home where Mrs. Curtis and I seemed always to have students under foot and anxious to talk of many things. There was always much to talk about after one had presented evolution as the historic fact, since the implications for religious orthodoxy were apparent.

In 1901, it seemed to me and to the vast majority of zoologists that the public controversy over evolution had ended a decade before the turn of the century. I remembered how, as a college student in the mid-nineties, I had almost wished that I had been born twenty years earlier and had participated in the Thirty Years' War (1859–89), when the fighting was really hot. If anyone had told me that within twenty-five years the fight would be on once more and the climax would be legislation against the teaching of a scientific fact so well established as the doctrine of evolution, this would have seemed incredible.

When, in the second decade of the present century, some of my former students, who had become teachers, began to report the restrictions laid upon them in high schools and in some of the denominational colleges, I was shocked indeed. Because such students had come to me with their problems and because the "Fundamentalist Crusade," under the leadership of William Jennings Bryan, was assuming alarming proportions, I began about 1920 to take an active part in the defense of evolution.

The fundamentalists were, of course, pressed for citations from reputable scientific sources in support of their contentions. Having no authoritative biologists of that day who would testify for special creation, they invoked such authorities as Georges Baron Cuvier, who died in 1832, or Louis Agassiz (1807–73), or little-known teachers in denominational colleges who were paraded as biologists of national reputation. Or the position of the individual quoted as not accepting evolution was incorrectly stated as in the case of a man named Etheridge who was cited as the director of the British Museum, whereas the authorities of this museum remembered him only as an obscure naturalist who had worked there for a short time and then gone they knew not where. Or the fundamentalists quoted some misunderstood statement by such an authority as W. Bateson, the great English geneticist, as evidence against evolution, whereas the meaning of the statement was quite the reverse. One such misrepresentation that was widely proclaimed was that Woodrow Wilson did not believe in evolution. The refutation of this malignment of the late President's intelligence appears in the letter addressed to me by Mr. Wilson as quoted in the statement I made for the record of the Scopes trial that went to the higher court. (See Appendix A.)

One wonders what the former President may have thought of his former Secretary of State, William Jennings Bryan, who was then leading the fundamentalist movement.

The Macedonian call from Dayton, Tennessee, that came to me one hot July morning in 1925 was probably due to my activities in defense of evolution as well as to my geographical location, to my recent book *Science and Human Affairs,* and to whatever standing I then had as a zoologist. The bubble of my conceit was punctured later when I learned that several of the then elder statesmen of zoology had been first solicited as witnesses by the American Civil Liberties Union but had made excuses of various sorts. In two such cases, as I learned later, the reason was that the trial would be only a piece of buffoonery and beneath the dignity of a zoologist of national reputation. The late Professor H. H. Newman and I, being zoologists of lesser standing, had no such concern for our dignity. And so, the experience at Dayton for him no doubt became, as it did for me, the most interesting of all our professional experiences of a general nature—one for which some of our seniors who might have gone to Dayton envied us in later years.

Arriving at Dayton in the late afternoon of Monday, July 13, I was met at the station by one of the younger scientists in attendance at the trial and driven to the quarters provided by the American Civil Liberties Union for our entertainment—a large house, known locally as The Mansion, once used by the owners of the nearly defunct Dayton Coal and Iron Company. This establishment, which had not been occupied for some years, had been made ready by George Rappleyea, one of the Dayton citizens most active in promoting the trial. Furniture, dishes and linen had been assembled; the plumbing was working again though it failed us at times; and servants had been provided.

After breakfast each morning we were driven to the courthouse; at noon we returned to The Mansion for lunch and were driven again to town for the afternoon session of the court. At night the lawyers came to The Mansion for dinner, and after the table was cleared we would continue talking over the events of the day and discussing the plans for the day following. It was here that I got my impressions of the lawyers for the defense.

Clarence Darrow was, of course, the "front" for our side, but it was evident that Arthur Garfield Hays was the manager. Dudley Field Malone impressed me as being more a politician than a lawyer, although he made some most effective speeches. John Randolph Neal, the Tennessee lawyer who stood with us, was evidently a man of caliber and principle.

For the prosecution William Jennings Bryan and his son were the only "foreign" lawyers in attendance. Although I had disagreed with Bryan's economic and social beliefs throughout his career, I came to regard him as an honest and conscientious idealist after hearing him give his famous lecture "A Conquering Nation" at the University of Missouri about 1904. And in 1912 when he was responsible more than anyone else for the Democratic convention's nomination of Woodrow Wilson, my respect for him was enhanced. Among the local attorneys for the prosecution, I remember vividly "General" Ben McKenzie who enlivened the trial by such declarations as, "We have done crossed the Rubicon."

In the courtroom it was evident that Judge John T. Raulston enjoyed himself tremendously as the commanding figure in a trial that was attracting worldwide attention. His deference to Mr. Bryan was obvious, and we all felt that his decisions day after day tended always to favor the prosecution. In illustration of this: when I was in line for my ticket home from Dayton, I overheard the agent, in conversation with a fellow Daytonian, remark, "I tell you Bryan's a great lawyer. He has not practiced for years, but did you notice how every time he made a point the Judge sustained him?"

Now, almost forty years later, as I read the stenographic record of the trial, it seems to me that Judge Raulston was not so partial as we thought. He was acting according to his lights as well as his prejudices. Since it was for him the greatest responsibility of his career to that time, who can blame him for being pleased to have his photograph taken so frequently. According to newspaper clippings that I have of his opinions toward the end of his life, he had then come to feel that such matters as the teaching of evolution were not proper subject matter for legal regulation. When I visited Dayton in the summer of 1956, I had an appointment, through Mr. Robinson the druggist, to meet Judge Raulston, but when we called at his homestead, we found he was "having a bad day" and that it was inadvisable for him to see any visitors. He died several days later.

John T. Scopes might well have seemed more than pleased with himself as the center of attraction; instead he was the acme of modesty. No man could have conducted himself better under the limelight. He impressed us as modest and without conceit though always ready to do his part. I thought of Scopes, when, in 1927, Charles A. Lindbergh stepped from his plane at the airport in Paris and, not realizing that a crowd awaited him, introduced himself by saying, "I am Charles Lindbergh and I have flown the Atlantic." John T. Scopes at Dayton was that kind of youngster.

Newspapermen were everywhere present and apparently having the time of their lives as they watched the passing show with characteristic cynicism.

The courtroom audience impressed me as mostly honest town and country folk in jeans and calico. "Boobs" perhaps, as judged by H. L. Mencken, with all the prejudices of backwoods Christian orthodoxy, but nevertheless a significant section of the backbone of democracy in the U.S.A. They came to see their idol, "The Great Commoner" and champion of the people, meet the challenge to their faith. They left bewildered but with their beliefs unchanged despite the manhandling of their idol by the "Infidel" from Chicago. Throughout the trial their frequent applause and "Amens," which Judge Raulston found impossible to control by threats of contempt or adjournment, showed that their hearts were with the prosecution. It did seem, however, that as the trial progressed they were coming to respect and even to like Clarence Darrow.

An item that I had never met in any of my reading regarding the trial came to me from Mr. Robinson, the druggist, during my visit to Dayton in the summer of 1956.

On the afternoon following Judge Raulston's adjournment of the court, which terminated Darrow's examination of his opponent, the feeling of the native population was intense. By nightfall the Dayton police, the sheriff's deputies, and the plainclothesmen—imported from Chattanooga to mingle with the crowd throughout the trial to better get the people's reactions than if they were known locally—were fearful of what might happen should Darrow resume his examination of Bryan the following morning. Someone with a squirrel rifle, from an upper window of a building across the way, could easily have picked Darrow off as he conducted his grilling of Bryan in the courthouse yard where court had been moved because of the heat.

As a result, these policing officers, according to Mr. Robinson, asked for an audience with the judge on the following day, an hour before the court was to convene. At this meeting Judge Raulston was told that, if the examination of Bryan were continued as planned, these officers could not be responsible for what might happen. The result was that when the court convened the judge expunged from the record all that had passed between Darrow and Bryan on the preceding day. The interchanges between the giants were thus removed from the legal record but not from the reporters' accounts that had gone on the wires nor from the ridicule of Mr. Bryan's cosmology that came back from around the world. He had known ridicule throughout his political career but never had his most cherished beliefs been held up to scorn. He appealed to the press for justice in the reporting of the address which he had intended to make to the court in explanation of his willingness to testify and in rebuttal of Mr. Darrow's questioning. Although this publicity was given in due course, its impact was overwhelmed by the news of Mr. Bryan's death a few days after the trial.

Such was my background before going to Dayton and the impression made upon me by the trial itself. But the present volume deals primarily with the impact of the Scopes trial through the years since 1925. In this connection I am asked to consider the statement (Appendix A) which I submitted for the record that went to the higher court.

Looking over this statement along with the comparable one by the late Horatio H. Newman, my fellow zoologist at the trial, I find them substantially what might have been expected in any authoritative textbook of general zoology in use by the better colleges and universities at that time. If a college textbook was weak in its account of evolution, one suspected that author and publisher were catering to the small denominational institutions.

The accounts of evolution in the two widely used textbooks in which Professor Newman and I had our respective interests are representative.[1] My own chapter, in the fourth edition of the Curtis and Guthrie textbook, is one of the most comprehensive of such accounts with which I am acquainted.[2] Today textbook chapters on

---

1 Horatio H. Newman, *Outlines of General Zoology* (New York: Macmillan Co., 1924).
2 Winterton C. Curtis and Mary J. Guthrie, *Textbook of General Zoology* (4th ed.; New York: John Wiley and Sons, Inc., 1947).

evolution tend to be somewhat reduced because the subject is so much an accepted fact. For example, when a leading oil company features dinosaurs in its advertising, one can assume that even children know that the animals of the past were not necessarily like those of the present, that the earth has been populated by animals and plants for millions of years, and that fossils are the remains of plants and animals that once lived and not objects created in the rocks by the Deity or by the Devil to confuse our understanding. The caveman as portrayed in the comics or by Walt Disney is another such example.

I do find that my reference to natural selection, which was first written while this doctrine was still somewhat under the critical reexamination it received in the first two decades of the present century, is somewhat more cautious than I would write today in a textbook chapter on evolution—now that natural selection has emerged triumphant as the most important directive factor in organic evolution.

As for the evidence in 1965 when compared with 1925, it has been but a confirmation and an amazing extension of the evidence for evolution as the historic fact and a more critical evaluation of theories concerning the directive factors involved in evolutionary change. In this connection, it is still important for the layman to understand the meaning of certain terms that have often confused thoughtful and intelligent individuals.

During the nineteenth century Darwin's name had become so linked with the word evolution that for the layman "Darwinism" and "evolution" were synonymous terms. For the biologist, on the other hand, Darwinism meant not necessarily evolution. More commonly Darwinism meant Darwin's theory of natural selection. During the nineties and the early twentieth century, when natural selection came under a critical reexamination, many laymen were misled by the statements of some biologists who criticized natural selection (sometimes calling it Darwinism) but with no thought of questioning evolution as the course of events in the story of life upon our planet. Although biologists became aware of this confusion and tried to correct it, there were many laymen, other than fundamentalists, who nevertheless believed that evolution had been rejected by some scientists of reputation. Thus, the fundamentalist crusaders received a degree of support from some of the more thoughtful members of the laity. Even today, fundamentalists sometimes have recourse to the claim that Darwinism has been rejected by scientists and, consequently, that evolution is a discredited theory. As a matter of fact, natural selection is now recognized as by far the most important factor involved in the direction of evolution and of no less importance than the heritable variations that are presented for selection. Such variations we now know to be carried by units in the germ cells known as genes.

In contrast with Darwin's scheme of natural selection, the Lamarckian theory of the inheritance of the effects of use and disuse and of environment and training upon the individual, and so upon the race by inheritance, have not been substantiated.

According to my memoranda, between 1923 and January, 1927, anti-evolution bills had been passed in two states and rejected in four others. In two states, resolutions by the legislatures and by the state school boards restricted the teaching of evolution and in three other states textbooks containing chapters on evolution had been barred from the public schools. Rulings by local boards of education outlawing the doctrine of evolution had become common especially in the South. As of January, 1927, campaigns to press anti-evolution bills for passage had been initiated in North Carolina, Arkansas, Washington, Minnesota, Missouri, North Dakota, Oregon, Kansas, Florida, and Virginia. These movements were backed by the Bible Crusaders, the Bryan Leaguers, the Fundamentalists Association, and all other well-financed organizations whose avowed objective was, "to put every teacher of evolution out of the tax-supported schools and colleges of America."

Although the trial at Dayton seemed to have given an impetus to the movement for such restrictive legislation, the net outcome of this furor must have been disappointing to the advocates of fundamentalism, since virtually all of the legislation pending in January, 1927, failed of enactment. By 1930, it was evident that the movement for such legislation had spent its force, although laws and restrictions by school boards were still on the books and enforced in many instances.

Thus, the Scopes trial seemed to put an end to attempts at restrictive legislation, because few individuals or organizations cared to face again the worldwide ridicule that would be forthcoming. Instead, the obscurantist activities were continued under cover. For example, one of my former students, who was then teaching in a Missouri high school, told me about 1940 that all books known to contain references to evolution had been secretly removed from the school library and that the librarian and the teachers likely to note such removals had been warned by the high school principal not to tell of these removals under penalty of dismissal.

In Missouri, during the thirties and forties, many students seemed to have been sensitized against evolution before coming to the state university. For example, one girl was reported as saying to one of my laboratory assistants, who had come from the same town: "When he began to lecture on evolution, I just sat back and laughed. I wasn't going to believe any of that stuff."

A common evasion, practiced by fundamentalist ministers even today, is to tell their young people that evolution was "discredited fifty years ago with the collapse of Darwinism." Thus, in the fall of 1953, the students in a class of Freshmen English at the University of Missouri were asked to write on some subject that was new to the individual and with which he or she had come in contact since coming to the university—any suitable subject presented in a course or as a campus problem. One student, who was taking zoology, chose evolution as her subject and presented a refutation along fundamentalist lines. Among other counts against evolution, she had one from her pastor at home, with whom she had discussed the matter and who had told her that he could not understand "why professors at the University of Missouri should still be teaching this exploded theory."

I'm not so sure that attempts at legislative repression may not come again. Listen to the "Good Old-time Religion" that pours from the radio on weekends, and even nightly. Evidently there are still plenty of fundamentalists who have not learned. The recent furor in Memphis, Tennessee, over evolution as too "controversial" a subject for teaching in a high school, shows where evolution stands in many schools and in states other than Tennessee.

On the hopeful side, I found among students a much greater interest in my course on evolution during the decade following 1925 while the "Monkey Trial" was still remembered. And so until my teaching ended in 1946, evolution seemed to be increasingly accepted among college students as a matter of course.

One wonders how long fundamentalism can maintain itself. The Protestant reactionaries would do well to take a lesson from their Roman Catholic contemporaries, who, as I understand it, now admit that evolution of this physical man has occurred. The Church thus renders unto Science the things that belong to Science. The Church deals with the spiritual man which is beyond the competence of Science—another example of the skill with which Catholicism can roll with the punch of advancing knowledge. Would that the funda-mentalists would learn that facts are stubborn things which will not be denied and that in the long run religious doctrines must square with the facts of science if these doctrines are to survive in the minds of educated and thoughtful men.

How extensive the stirrings of orthodox theology may have be-come and will continue to be as a result of the Scopes trial I cannot say. My contacts with such theology have been limited except as it comes to me by radio when I practice my habit of listening to opinions with which I disagree. This I dislike doing, in theological matters, because it tends to make me feel superior and I dislike feeling that way—it seems too much like snobbery. By and large, I do not think the outlook particularly encouraging for the triumph of sense over nonsense. The concept of the present book, arising as it did from a theological source, is heartening. I shall await the public reaction, orthodox and unorthodox, with interest.

My hope for the ultimate acceptance of the doctrine of evolution and the adjustment of theological doctrine thereto is based on my confidence in the ultimate triumph of reason with respect to the popular acceptance of scientific facts. Such acceptance comes slowly when cherished idols of popular belief are involved. But it does come. How many educated people now believe that the earth is flat or that the sun goes around the earth as it seems to do? A favorite quotation of mine in this connection is from Andrew D. White:

There came, one after the other, five of the greatest men our race has produced—Copernicus, Kepler, Galileo, Descartes, and Newton—and when their work was done the old theological conception of the Universe was gone. The spacious firmament on high—"the crystalline spheres"—the Almighty enthroned upon "the circle of the heavens," and with his own hands, or with angels as his agents, keeping sun, moon and planets in motion for the benefit of the earth, opening and closing the "windows of heaven" letting down upon the earth the "waters above the firmament," setting his bow in the cloud, hanging out "signs and wonders," hurling comets, "casting forth lightnings" to scare the wicked, and "shaking the earth" in his wrath: all this had disappeared.[3]

The reconciliation between the biblical account of creation and the facts of biological science is, after all, one to be effected by the

3 Andrew D. White, *A History of the Warfare of Science with Theology in Christendom* (New York: D. Appleton and Co., 1910).

theologians. Today the liberals in theology seem to be on the increase. It is for them, not for the scientist, to carry on.

My confidence that the concept of organic evolution will win as have the concepts of a solar centric system and a spherical earth is based upon my confidence in man's intelligence once the facts are viewed unclouded by too many preconceptions. Despite the delayed acceptance of the doctrine of evolution in conservative religious circles, I believe that the impact of the Scopes trial has been at work. In the end those July days at Dayton in 1925 may indeed be recognized as "D-Days" in the warfare of science against outworn theological doctrines.

As for the impact of the Scopes trial upon the scientists in attendance, I can speak only for myself. For me those days at Dayton were the most far-reaching of all my professional experiences.

My mental state when I went to Dayton was such that I was perhaps more in need of the inspiration I received from Mr. Darrow than I realized. In the spring of 1920 a duodenal ulcer and in 1923 a severe recurrence had brought me nearer to the Death Angel than I liked to think. At Dayton I was still inconvenienced by the necessity of a glass of milk in midmorning, midafternoon, and at bedtime. Then, in the spring of 1924 I had been told that I had perhaps two years to live. A growth diagnosed as Hodgkin's disease had been removed from my neck, and the diagnosis originating at the University of Missouri School of Medicine had been confirmed at the Mayo Clinic, at the Johns Hopkins Medical School, at the Northwestern University Medical School, and by a pathologist of note in California. Although mine was the earliest case the Mayo Clinic had ever seen, all the authorities agreed in their diagnoses. At age forty-eight, when I had just assumed important professional responsibilities and had new hopes for my research program, this was indeed a problem for me and for my family. But I found my agnostic philosophy of life sufficient unto the day and set to work upon one of the Curtis and Guthrie textbooks which were later published in four editions and are still carried on by my successors. My escape was in work that took my mind off my problem, my philosophy that we all take our chances with the order of nature and that this problem was mine to handle as best I could without hope of Heaven or fear of Hell. Now, I am frequently told, "If you had Hodgkin's and got well, you didn't have it." To which I reply, "Well, I had all the thrills."

In our talk around the table after dinner that first night at Dayton, I must have said something that interested Mr. Darrow for as we left the table, he and I continued the conversation and sitting down alone on the veranda of The Mansion continued our talk until almost midnight. When we parted he remarked, "There aren't many who think about these things as you and I do. It's too bad we can't see each other often." Although I felt complimented by this remark, the important thing I got from this first contact with Darrow was an uplift of spirit. It seemed to me I could still keep going—"full speed ahead and damn the torpedoes." I remember writing him some weeks after the trial, "Because of meeting you, I have renewed courage to face life and now I can never be really lonely again."

We met perhaps a dozen or more times after 1925, and I have a handful of letters from Darrow, mostly scrawled in longhand, which are among my most cherished possessions. Once, when we had missed a meeting, he wrote, "I cannot see you often enough in the little time that remains," and in his inditement of his book *Farmington,* which he sent me, he wrote, "In memory of one of the richest friendships I ever formed."

The title, *World's Most Famous Court Trial,* given to an account of the Scopes trial is no doubt an exaggeration.[4] Yet this trial will long be remembered as a major episode in the conflict between scientific and theological viewpoints. For one who participated in this trial, it is a story to be told to his grandchildren and for these grandchildren to remember.

Never shall I forget the impression made upon me by the city of Peiping which I visited in December, 1932, on a vacation from my year as a visiting professor at Keiogijuku University in Tokyo. For years after I would find myself saying in memory, "I saw Peiping— I saw Peiping." Now that I realize their historic import, I am saying, "I saw D-Days at Dayton."

4 *The World's Most Famous Court Trial: Tennessee Evolution Trial* (Cincinnati, Ohio: National Book Company, 1925). This volume is taken directly from the court record of the trial.

GEOLOGY AND GENESIS

KIRTLEY F. MATHER

K IRTLEY F. MATHER received his Ph.D. in geology from the University of Chicago in 1915. After serving on the faculties of several universities he went to Harvard where he remained until 1954, when he became Professor of Geology, Emeritus. He has served on the general board of the National Council of Churches, as vice-president of the Institute on Religion in an Age of Science, and as a member of the Society for the Scientific Study of Religion. Invited to testify for the defense in the Scopes case, he, like Professor Curtis, never took the stand.

The attorneys and witnesses for the defense of John T. Scopes in July, 1925, went to Dayton, Tennessee, with three purposes in mind. First, to lay the foundations for an appeal to higher courts after his conviction, in the hope that the Tennessee statute forbidding the teaching of evolution in the schools of that state would eventually be "struck down" as unconstitutional legislation. Secondly, to present to the court and through mass media to the world at large the factual basis for the doctrine of evolution and the far-reaching importance of that doctrine in science. And, thirdly, to set before the same audience the argument that the theory of evolution is not destructive of the spiritual and moral values of enduring religious principles in the biblical accounts of creation. I welcome this opportunity, forty years after the trial, to review what was said and done at that time, in the light of the remarkable progress in knowledge and understanding during these years.

It should be noted first that the defense failed in its appeal to the Supreme Court of Tennessee, not because of any shortcomings in the conduct of the trial but because of an unsuspected technicality in the Tennessee legal complex. It is a story worth telling. In the closing minutes of the trial, Judge Raulston instructed the jury that if they found the defendant guilty and were "content with the specified minimum fine of $100" they could "leave the punishment to the Court." Whereupon Attorney General Stewart rose from his place among the attorneys for the prosecution and secured the judge's permission to address the court: "Of course, your honor, it is a minor matter, but I had it in mind that it would be the duty of the jury to fix whatever fine was imposed." The judge replied that "the Court can always impose the minimum fine under a statute" and then went on at some length to compare the trial then in progress with the many bootlegging trials at which he had presided and at which he always assessed the fine of $100. Before he had finished, Mr. Stewart resumed his seat in silence. In retrospect, that was the most dramatic of the many dramatic episodes in the entire trial, although none of us recognized it as such at the time. When the case eventually reached the Supreme Court of Tennessee, that court reversed the judgment of the circuit court because Judge Raulston "had been in error in imposing a fine greater than $50 without having the amount of the fine determined by the jury," or words to that effect. It would seem to me that the youthful, keen-minded, alert Attorney General, easily the most knowledgeable of all the lawyers in the courtroom concerning the statutes of his state, had instinctively leaped to his feet to stop Judge Raulston from committing that error. Then, as the judge rambled on, the thought may well have occurred to him that this technical error would make it unnecessary for the higher court to pass upon the constitutionality of the statute and chastise the state legislature by finding it unconstitutional, as he probably expected that court would have to do. Such in fact was the result. The case was remanded to the lower court for retrial, and at the same time it was indicated that no useful purpose could be served by trying it again.

There the matter rests. The anti-evolution law is still in the Tennessee statutes, its constitutionality unresolved. Apparently, no steps were ever taken to bring John Scopes into court for a second trial, and certainly no one else has ever been indicted for violating this law. There is, however, no way to ascertain how many timid teachers in obscure hamlets among the Tennessee hills have avoided all references to evolution in their classrooms because that law hangs over their heads like a sword of Damocles.

In contrast to the failure of the defense to achieve the first of the three objectives set forth above, the success attained in its educational endeavor was truly remarkable. When Judge Raulston ruled that any testimony that might be offered by the so-called expert witnesses from the scientific disciplines would be irrelevant and that they could not take the witness stand, the defense objected so strenuously that he agreed to include in the record of the case written statements setting forth the testimony they wanted to present, in order that the higher court could determine on appeal whether or not his ruling was legally correct. Court was adjourned at noon on Friday, July 17, to resume the following Monday morning, at which time the affidavits were to be presented for the record. Typewriters and mimeograph machines were put into action, telegraph wires hummed, and under the dateline, "Dayton, Tenn., July 20," large segments of those voluminous statements appeared in hundreds of newspapers throughout the world.

During the summer of 1925, I was employed as a consulting geologist by one of the larger American petroleum corporations for an exploratory survey of Cape Breton Island, Nova Scotia, to appraise the possibilities of finding oil in commercial quantities there. I did not want to be away from my remunerative job any longer than necessary, and the American Civil Liberties Union had informed me that I would not be needed in Dayton until the fifth or sixth day of the trial. Accordingly I arrived there on Saturday morning, July 18, to be immediately ensconced behind a typewriter. By late afternoon the next day, my contribution to the Scopes trial was ready for the mimeographers. It is this statement, hastily prepared in 1925, that I want now to review in the light of whatever knowledge and insight I have in 1964.

With all due modesty, I must confess that when I read that statement (Appendix B) after the lapse of more than three decades I felt the glow of pride that I had done so well. Of course, my presentation of the factual data of geologic life development was couched in such general terms that even the discovery of thousands of species of fossil animals and plants, unknown in 1925, could hardly say me nay. Many of those newly discovered fossils fill in the gaps in our earlier knowledge about the sequence of life in the history of the earth. Some of them require changes in our thinking about certain relatively minor details pertaining to the evolution of extinct or living plants and animals. But the broad panorama of progressively more modern inhabitants of the earth during the successive periods of geologic time remains pretty much the same as it appeared to be in 1925. And the fact that the living creatures at any time or place were the descendants of previously existing animals or plants, often changed in response to the processes of evolution, is even more certain now than then.

There are, however, some notable corrections that should be made in my 1925 statement. Their significance is more apparent than real; they have little or no bearing upon the doctrine of evolution; nevertheless they should be made to keep the record true. The advancing knowledge of nuclear physics has now made available a number of radioactive timekeepers—uranium-lead, potassium-argon, carbon-14 —which have been put to good use by geologists. The result has been to lengthen considerably the geologic time-scale and to increase greatly the accuracy with which past events can be dated in terms of years.

Consequently, my statement, "In the very oldest rocks which have yet been discovered which are at least one hundred million years old, there are absolutely no traces whatsoever of any animal or plant life," should be corrected to read, "which are at least fifteen hundred million years old and some of which date back as far as three billion years ago." Similarly, the Paleozoic era, with its remarkable record of the successive appearance of the first fishes, then of the primitive amphibians, and later of the ancestral reptiles, would now be described as beginning about six hundred million years ago (rather than "at least fifty million years ago") and terminating about two hundred and twenty-five million years ago. It was followed by the Mesozoic era which continued until approximately seventy million years ago, the date now attributed to the beginning of the Cenozoic era (rather than "five or ten million years ago").

Using the new methods for measuring time, it is now possible to date the advent of the first primitive mammals (egg-laying or marsupial) at approximately a hundred and fifty million years ago and the first appearance of placental mammals (those whose young are born after a considerable period of gestation in the womb of the mother) at approximately ninety million years ago. The first primates (the order of placental mammals that includes the lemurs, the tarsiers, the monkeys, the apes, and mankind) appeared in the fossil record about sixty million years ago; the first anthropoids (the subdivision of the primates that includes apes and men but excludes the lemurs, tarsiers, and monkeys) about thirty million years ago; and the first hominids (the family of mankind) between fifteen and five million years ago.

The wide spread of that last date is due not so much to lack of precision in determining the age of the relevant fossils as to uncertainty concerning the biological relationships of the creatures represented by those fossils. In the last thirty years, hundreds of fossils representing extinct species of anthropoids have been found in Africa (especially in Kenya and Tanganyika) and Asia (especially in the Siwalik Hills of India, in Pakistan, and in eastern China) in geological formations ranging in age from thirty million to a half-million years. Some of these fossils can be referred by the experts without hesitation to an extinct group of apes known as the dryopithecines, so generalized in body structure and tooth pattern that they apparently include the progenitors both of man and the great apes of Africa and Borneo. Others are referred with equal confidence to an extinct group of hominids known as the australopithecines, so specialized in body structure and tooth pattern that they must have been in the ancestral lineage of modern man. Still others, however, have characteristics that divide the experts into two camps: some would regard them as advanced pongids (apes), others as primitive hominids. The transitional nature of these specimens (the most important of which were found in India and Kenya and are now referred to the genus Ramapithecus) reinforces the belief, widely held by anthropologists and paleontologists, that man evolved from apelike ancestors in East Africa and South Asia during the last ten million years of earth history. Thence, Stone Age man spread to Europe, other parts of Africa and Asia, and eventually to North and South America and Australia.

Several important discoveries of relics of prehistoric man have recently been made in North America. These, combined with the new technique of carbon-14 dating, indicate that human beings first reached the southern half of this continent between twenty-five and thirty thousand years ago, rather than "not more than ten or twelve thousand years ago," as I stated in 1925. Still it is true, however, that "the oldest human inhabitants of North America were members of the existing races of mankind."

Much progress has also been made toward solving the problem of the origin of life on our planet, despite the fact that there is even less expectation now than in 1925 that "a direct record of whence came the first living cell" will ever be found. But the chemical processes whereby a living cell could be synthesized from previously existing inorganic matter are much better understood today than then. And the belief that the first primitive forms of life evolved from the material ingredients and energy resources available at the earth's surface and in its water bodies a couple billion years ago is even more firmly established.

The only change I would now make in my 1925 statement concerning the origin of life would be to qualify the implication that all forms of plant and animal life had evolved from the same "first living cell." The development of a living cell from its nonliving antecedents may have occurred at many places and at different times, before the earth was so thoroughly populated with hungry bacteria, bacteriophages, and protozoans that the long sequence of chemical synthesis could never again be completed. The emergence of the living from the non-living is possible only in an absolutely sterile environment, but all the earth was sterile until the primitive unicellular plants and animals had multiplied and spread around its surface. It is therefore quite likely that the synthesis of a molecule or a molecular organization of the requisite composition and complexity to enable it to assimilate nourishment, grow, and replicate itself was not a unique event. Some of the differences between the many varied, one-celled creatures are probably due to differences in the biochemical organization of the various "first living cells" from which they descended. Among those differences may well have been those that made possible the creative evolution of the progressive multicellular invertebrates from certain protozoans, whereas the descendants of other ancestral protozoans have remained protozoans to the present day.

All of which is to say that, insofar as the doctrine of evolution is based upon knowledge about geologic phenomena, this doctrine is even more firmly established in 1965 than in 1925. Moreover, many details of the process of geologic life development are better known today than then.

But my own interest in the trial of John Scopes was stimulated more by the third objective of those who participated in his defense than by the second. When I learned from the newspapers that William Jennings Bryan was going to Dayton to aid in the prosecution of the defendant and denounce evolution as an enemy of Christianity and that Clarence Darrow was going there to aid in the defense of the youthful schoolteacher and cross swords with the man whose religious beliefs he rejected, I wondered who would be there to defend a religion that was intellectually respectable in the light of modern science. The fact that the Tennessee legislature had passed the anti-evolution law was evidence enough that too many people had accepted the spellbinding orator's assertion that "you cannot believe both in evolution and in God." In this twentieth-century recrudescence of the nineteenth-century warfare between science and theology, it would not suffice merely to promote science and demolish medieval theology. Religion was more in need of protection from those who thought mistakenly they were its friends than from the "agnostics, atheists, and infidels," against whom Mr. Bryan was so vociferous.

Consequently I had gotten in touch with Roger Baldwin of the American Civil Liberties Union to suggest that, in mobilizing the presumably eminent expert witnesses for the defense, scientists should be selected who were not only held in esteem by their fellow-scientists but were also active members of a church and in good standing in a religious denomination. I told him that I was at that time a deacon in the First Baptist Church of Newton, Massachusetts, and the teacher of an adult class in its church school. I opened wide the door for an invitation to participate in the forthcoming trial; I may even have explicitly volunteered my services. (I cannot find the correspondence in my files and I am here depending solely on memory.) In any event, that was the start of the chain of circumstances leading to my presence in Dayton and the preparation of the statement here under review.

More than a third of that statement was devoted to the propositions that the scientific doctrine of evolution neither contradicts the biblical record of creation when intelligently interpreted nor destroys the fundamental principles of valid religion. This part of my statement was most extensively quoted or otherwise used by the reporters who summarized and excerpted for their newspapers and wire services the several statements made available to them. Evidently many of them agreed with me that a knowledgeable person may consistently believe both in evolution and in God and that "to say that one must choose between evolution and Christianity is exactly like telling the child as he starts for school that he must choose between spelling and arithmetic."

The changes I would now make in that part of my forty-year-old statement are all in the nature of emphasis or of amplification rather than of correction. Discussing the relation between the modern concept of evolution and the biblical accounts of creation, I stated that "evolution is a process, a method," whereas "God is a power, a force." That idea may well be enlarged to stress the fundamental difference between the approach of the scientist and that of the religionist to the problems pertaining to the origin and history of man, of all living creatures, of the earth, the solar system, the universe. The scientist seeks answers to the question *how* did things come to be as they are, by what processes were the world and man created. The religionist seeks answers to the question *why* did things come to be as they are, for what purposes were the world and man created. Men need trustworthy answers to both kinds of questions; upon those answers depend the physical, mental, and spiritual welfare of each individual human being and of mankind collectively.

The first chapter of Genesis is a sober, straightforward attempt to answer the religious question in the light of the little that was known about the nature of the world and man during the twentieth to fifteenth centuries B.C. in the region between the Mediterranean Sea and the Persian Gulf. "And God saw every thing that he had made, and, behold, it was very good." But there is also a suggestion of an effort to answer the scientific question as well. The patriarchs of that ancient time and place were sufficiently impressed with the orderliness of nature that they explained what they knew in terms of an orderly sequence of creative events under administrative regulation. The order of events is now known to have been quite different from what they thought. There were "lights in the firmament of the heaven" long before "the waters were gathered together in the seas"; the lower forms of animal life were present long before the seed-bearing plants appeared. But these are relatively unimportant details. The truly significant and long-lasting contribution to the advance of knowledge is the recognition of the fact that the world in which we live is under some kind of an administration. This is an idea that is fundamental in every scientific enterprise today. The more we learn about evolution, the more convinced are we that it is an orderly process of change, operating in accordance with administrative regulations.

To be sure, there is a large factor of uncertainty in the behavior of such subatomic entities as electrons. But just as soon as electrons, protons, and neutrons are organized to become atoms, they display meticulous obedience to regulations that are being spelled out with ever-increasing exactness by the physicists and chemists of today. Witness the mathematical elegance of the periodic table of the elements and the exquisite precision with which atoms are changed by radioactive decay. Had Jesus been conversing with a group of modern college students, he might well have added to his sage advice, "Consider the lilies of the field, how they grow," the equally profound suggestion, "Give thought to the atoms and how they change."

It is also true that many—perhaps most—of the "laws of nature" are statistical laws, dealing with the behavior of aggregations of many individuals each of which seems to act at random, such as the regulations pertaining to gases or those concerning genetics discovered by Mendel and his followers. But statistical laws are no less binding; they, like other manifestations of rational—that is, comprehensible by reasoning minds—transformations of matter and energy tell us much about the nature of the administration of the universe.[1]

The theologian should note, however, that this scientific term, "the administration of the universe," is not written with a capital A; nor may he assume that "administration" is synonymous with "Administrator." In the vocabulary of science, it is simply the designation for that—whatever that may be—which determines the orderly sequence of change in the measurable aspects of the universe in space and time. It is the responsibility of the theologian, not of the scientist, to ascertain whether the administration of the universe has characteristics or qualities that validate such designations as the "God of Justice and Mercy" proclaimed by Micah or the "Heavenly Father" to whom Jesus prayed. In fulfilling this responsibility the theologian should not expect any assistance from the astronomer or the physicist in their professional capacities. The biologist may give him some clues; the psychologist, the anthropologist, and the sociologist may be of some help; but he must go beyond the pale of science and deal specifically with the spiritual aspects of life if he is to succeed.

Such thoughts as these were evidently beginning to form in my

1 The writer has dealt at greater length with these and related ideas in an essay entitled "Creation and Evolution," in Harlow Shapley (ed.), *Science Ponders Religion* (New York: Appleton Century Crofts, 1960).

mind when I included in my 1925 statement the following sentences:
"The facts ascertained by natural science are obviously incomplete;
the record of the rocks by no means tells the whole story. Man not
only has an efficient and readily adaptable body; he also possesses a
knowledge of moral law, a sense of rightness, a confidence that his
reasoning mind finds response in a rational universe, and a hope
that his spiritual aspirations will find increasing answer in a spiritual
universe. Such things as these cannot be preserved in the fossil
record, yet their presence must be accounted for."

Interestingly enough, the authors of the biblical accounts of creation
were concerned with some of these things too. The story of the
Garden of Eden, beginning with Genesis 2:4 and continuing to the
end of the third chapter, is quite different from the account that
precedes it, but it also has significant insights. In this case they
pertain to the nature of man rather than to the administration of the
universe. (Anyone who reads thoughtfully the last three verses of
Genesis 3 cannot fail to observe how faulty is its concept of the
nature of God when compared to that of the later Hebrew prophets
and of Jesus.) This is obviously an allegory, a parable, or a fable,
written with poetic imagination and fervor rather than with scientific
objectivity and poise. When anyone talks or writes about a garden in
which are a "tree of life" and a "tree of knowledge of good and evil,"
he does not expect to be taken literally, any more than Jesus did when
he told his companions that they were "the salt of the earth."

Far back in the evolutionary development of mankind, some unknown ancestor of ours first flaked a flint to a cutting edge and thus
began a type of behavior eventually demonstrating that *Homo sapiens,*
man the thinker, is also *Homo faber,* man the maker. Fully as significant, there must also have been someone in our ancestral lineage who
first said it would be wrong to do that, right to do this—one who had
"eaten the fruit of the tree of knowledge of good and evil." And it
probably *was* a female of the species who first became aware of the
reality of moral law and its significance for human welfare. As soon
as this awareness was shared by others in the clan, there was a
disposition to act according to moral principles in purposeful ways
designed to achieve desirable goals. In all probability this emergence
of a distinctively human trait from subhuman animal characteristics
was closely associated in time and place with the emergence of self-
consciousness from the antecedent consciousness of one's surround-
ings; "and they knew that they were naked."

There has been much progress since 1925 in accounting for man's
"hope that his spiritual aspirations will find increasing answer in a
spiritual universe." Moreover, from a strictly scientific viewpoint, that
hope now appears far more reasonable than it did then. Scientists are
seeking to make as intimate intellectual contact with ultimate reality
as possible; they now tell us that there is a nonmaterial universe "behind" the world of sense perception. Matter is a local and temporary
expression of energy; energy is a manifestation of "force fields." The
best known of these fields of force are the gravitational and the
electromagnetic; a nuclear force field is also beginning to be recognized
and others presumably await discovery. In a force field there is action
at a distance. "Field potential is at all times present at every point,
inside and around every atom, thing, creature, and process." [2] Fields
are universal, virtually infinite, presumably eternal; they display
internal consistency and are therefore intelligible; they come as near
to being ultimate causes as the mind can grasp. They cannot be
directly experienced by sense perception, but their reality is now
beyond challenge.

Apply this new and thought-provoking concept of the fundamental
nature of the universe to the problems of organic evolution. Primitive
one-celled creatures, immersed in water, make no response to gravitation. For them, the consciousness of up or down, east or west, is
irrelevant to the continuity of existence. When sufficiently complex
multicellular creatures appeared, that field could no longer be ignored.
To maintain their position in the water or propel their bodies in a
desired direction, primitive fish developed fins and a sense of balance;
these were a response to the force potential of the all-pervading gravitational field. Any land animal that moves itself by means of loco-
motor organs has adapted to gravitation. We human beings can
walk, run, jump, and climb because our remote ancestors long ago
responded to the gravitational field; their evolution involved adjust-
ments of their bodies and behavior in accordance with its directives.

Similarly the first forms of animal life, like many of the less
complexly organized invertebrates of today, were unaware that they
were living in an electromagnetic field, or at least they displayed no
response to its presence. Gradually, however, in the course of evolution, light-sensitive epidermal cells came into existence and some of

2 F. L. Kunz, "The Reality of the Non-Material," *Main Currents in Modern
Thought*, XX (1963), 33–40.

these developed into eyes of various degrees of perfection. Certain creatures, capable of doing so, had become adjusted to that portion of the electromagnetic spectrum which we call light.

To account for man's spiritual aspirations, it is not illogical to postulate the presence of a spiritual field among the universal fields of force, analogous in many ways to those to which our ancestors had thus responded. The force potential of this field would be such as to impel in creatures capable of response an awareness of "the beauty of the sunset and the glory of the dawn," a desire to "know the truth," a sensitivity to justice and righteousness, a recognition of the fact that life may be something more than mere existence. In this manner the human spirit would emerge in the process of creative evolution as a response to the spiritual realities in the universe.

This idea that man—the whole man: body, mind, and spirit—is a product of evolutionary processes emphasizes the necessity for mutual understanding and close cooperation between scientists and religionists. But it confronts them with many perplexing problems in their endeavors to contribute to human welfare. I tried to deal with some of those problems in my 1925 statement when I wrote: "To many, evolution means the survival of the fittest in the struggle for existence; and that is taken to imply that the selfish triumph, the most cruel and bloodthirsty are exalted, those who disregard others win. Obviously this is the very antithesis of Christianity" with its "teaching that the law of life is love, that service to others is the true guiding principle, that self-sacrifice even to death is the best trait a man can display."

To resolve that moral dilemma, I went on to point out that this interpretation of the "survival of the fittest" is erroneous. "At times of crisis in the past it was rarely selfishness or cruelty or strength of talon and of claw that determined success or failure. Survival values at different times have been measured in different terms. Ability to breathe air by means of lungs rather than purify the blood by means of gills meant success in escaping from the water to the land. Love of offspring and tender care for the young gave the weak and puny mammals of long ago the ability to triumph over much stronger and more powerful reptiles. . . . Especially in the strain that leads to man can we note the increasing spread of habits of cooperation, of unselfishness, of love."

Much more is known today about such matters than in 1925. Books have been written by competent authorities about the role of mutual aid in organic evolution.[3] Important studies have been made concerning the internal organization of congregations of gregarious wild animals, such as herds of antelope, companies of baboons, prides of lions, packs of wolves. Animals often behave quite differently in the wild than in the zoo or when domesticated. Information about the widely publicized "pecking order" among barnyard fowl is not nearly so relevant as knowledge concerning parental care of young and the functions of leadership and territorial rights among chimpanzees in the forest.

Our pithecine ancestors lived in jungles and on grassy steppes. They obeyed the "law of the jungle." The men of the Old Stone Age inherited many of their mental habits and emotional traits. They too were "killers"; most of the tools recovered by cultural anthropologists from ancient archeological sites are weapons. And men who display Old Stone Age patterns of behavior are still with us today. How can the modern Christian, Jew, Hindu, or Muslim deal with his own animal heritage and that of his fellows?

Fortunately we know a great deal more about the "law of the jungle" today than did Kipling when he equated it with the primacy of "fang and claw." Robert Ardrey has described it in his vivid prose [4] as a combination of "enmity-amity"—enmity toward those outside one's own congregation, amity toward those within it. The history of mankind during the last half-million years has been marked by increasingly efficient organization of individuals in social groups on an amicable basis and by progressive expansion of the "territory" within which amity is sovereign. Families banded together into clans, clans joined to form tribes, tribes united to create nations, and today the dream of a "federation of the world, a parliament of man," has a much greater possibility of achievement than ever before. Our heritage from jungle-dwelling ancestors of the goodly ingredient called amity is a potential vital force which only needs to be brought to full fruition, liquidating the heritage of enmity in its rise to sovereignty, in order to realize the prophets' dreams of a terrestrial "City of God." And in that process it should always be remembered that there must be effective amity within the boundary circle of enmity-amity

---

3 P. Kropotkin, *Mutual Aid, A Factor in Evolution* (New York: Knopf, 1914); W. C. Allee, *Cooperation Among Animals* (New York: Schuman, 1951); Caryl P. Haskins, *Of Societies and Men* (New York: Norton, 1951).

4 Robert Ardrey, *African Genesis* (New York: Atheneum Press, 1961).

before that circle can be enlarged to embrace additional "territory."

Fortunately also, we are today recognizing more clearly than in 1925 the distinction between cultural evolution and biological evolution. These matters of interpersonal and intergroup relations are cultural aspects of life, as are also the deeper inner thoughts one has about his personal relations to the universe and its administration. Man's body, probably even including his brain, is now more or less stabilized. Certainly we are doing all we can to standardize it, by means of modern programs of public health, beauty contests, athletic competitions, etc., on an international as well as a local basis. But the spirit of man is still struggling in travail. Man's cultural evolution has just begun; its possibilities for future progress are literally beyond measure. Surely, in this critical moment in cosmic history, when man has just about fulfilled the ancient directive to "be fruitful and multiply and replenish the earth and subdue it," emphasis must be placed upon his further cultural evolution.

Fortunately, again, the tempo of cultural evolution, whether progressive or retrogressive, is very much more rapid than that of biological evolution. Changes in organs and structures in the body can be transmitted to offspring only if they are the results of prior changes in the genes, the "carriers" of inheritable characteristics. Consequently, biological evolution is slow, even in the perspective of geological time. In contrast, knowledge and emotions, ideas and ideals acquired by one generation may be transmitted immediately and directly to the next generation. It is the function of science not only to extend knowledge but also to screen out from the transmission line any faulty ideas. It is the function of religion to screen out unworthy ideals and promote the transmission of emotions that bind men together.

Toward the end of my 1925 statement, I find the following sentences: "Men of science have as their aim the discovery of facts. They seek truth with open eyes, willing to recognize it, as Huxley said, even if 'it sears the eyeballs.' After they have discovered truth, and not till then, do they consider what its moral implications may be. . . . Men of religion seek righteousness; finding it they also find truth. The farther along the two avenues of investigation the scientist and the theologian go, the closer together they discover themselves to be. Already many of them are marching shoulder to shoulder in their endeavor to combine a trained and reasoning mind with a faithful and loving heart in every human individual and thus to develop more perfectly in mankind the image of God. Neither the right kind of mind nor the right kind of heart will suffice without the other. Both are needed, if civilization is to be saved."

Philosophically minded scientists and prophetically minded theologians are indeed closer together today than they were when I wrote those lines. Both have moved forward considerable distances along their avenues of investigation toward a truer, fuller, and more valuable understanding of the nature of the universe, of its administration, and of its human inhabitants.

The model of the universe which the scientist constructs in his mind has been drastically changed. The new concepts of fields of force are only part of the story. The mechanistic materialism that seemed so soundly based upon the scientific knowledge current in the latter half of the nineteenth century and the first decade or two of the twentieth has been largely discarded. That effects are predetermined by causes is still a guiding principle in many narrowly defined research projects, but "operational research" is superseding it in many others. The true nature of causality and determinism is under critical examination and no completely satisfactory answers have yet been given to many of the questions raised by its consideration. The limitations of science as well as its conquests are now widely recognized. Certainly, the "world view" of modern science provides a much more secure and hospitable foundation upon which theologians may rear their superstructure of faith and reverence than did that of nineteenth-century science.

Similarly the description of God which a modern theologian might try to present—he would probably begin correctly by saying that God is ineffable—is drastically different from that given by most of the church fathers of preceding centuries. Theological doctrines that are intellectually respectable in the light of modern science have superseded many of the ancient dogmas. Biblical exegesis has moved far away from the literalistic historicity of medieval orthodoxy. Scientifically based principles of psychological and psychiatric counseling are increasingly employed in the confessional, the minister's study, and the rabbi's sanctum. More significantly, there is now a widespread recognition of the idea that the "revelations" of religion have much in common with the "discoveries" of science; they are essentially two different labels for a human experience in a moment of insight. And of equal significance, the percentage of religious leaders who emphasize "the social gospel" in their activities is far greater than it was when that term was first coined.

The two avenues have closely converged, but the dual highway stretches far ahead. Civilization has not yet been saved. The amount of hope one may have for the future depends upon the willingness of men to accept responsibility for further progress. It is encouraging to note that the cultural evolution of the last ten thousand years is the latest (but not necessarily the last) culmination of orderly processes of change taking place throughout immeasurably long ages in accordance with administrative regulations. "As the twig is bent, so is the tree inclined." But it is necessary to note also that evolution has only occasionally meant onward and upward to ever higher and better things. "Many are called, but few are chosen." Evolution has never guaranteed success; it only provides opportunity for success.

Mankind today has a unique opportunity to achieve a destiny made possible by billions of years of cosmic and organic evolution, a destiny delineated by projecting into the future the trend of past geologic life development. But mankind will succeed in capitalizing upon that opportunity, or fail to take advantage of it, precisely as men, individually and collectively, determine.

I doubt if I would have put it quite that way in 1925, and I am sure that the courtroom in which John T. Scopes was being tried would not have been the best time and place to do so, even if I had wanted to. But that is the way I see it today.

CURRENT THOUGHTS
ON BIOLOGICAL EVOLUTION

LAMONT C. COLE

L AMONT C. COLE holds a B.S. in physics, an M.S. in biology, and a Ph.D. in zoology. After completing his schooling, he served as a commissioned officer with the U.S. Public Health Service for two years; then he returned to the academic world to teach zoology. He is presently chairman of the Department of Zoology at Cornell University. Although a young boy at the time of the Dayton trial, he remembers his father's participation in it as one of the scientists called for the defense.

Wednesday, July 15, 1925, was my ninth birthday. On that day Judge John T. Raulston, sitting on the bench in Dayton, Tennessee, denied a defense motion to quash the indictment against John T. Scopes, and ordered the trial to continue.

My father was absent from my birthday celebration because he had been in Dayton for the past few days. My mother and I were with my maternal grandparents in Plano, Illinois, and for the next several days we were to spend long hours listening to two pairs of "earphones" connected in series by means of a rubber band and plugged into a radio equipped with a full-size storage battery to heat the filament of its single tube. The radio was firmly tuned to the Chicago *Tribune* station, WGN (for "World's Greatest Newspaper"), which was setting a precedent by giving what is now called "live coverage" to such a thing as a court trial.

My father died on September 3, 1961, but I shall try to tell here what the trial meant to him. He has left me voluminous notes, manuscripts, files of newspaper clippings, and memories of a long, close association which included many discussions of the Dayton trial. It may be instructive to tell what sort of man he was who, in 1925, was to be publicly called a "heretic" and to inspire a Southern Baptist Convention to write the president of the University of Chicago describing him as "a snake in the grass corrupting the youth of the nation."

My paternal grandfather was a Methodist minister and one of the founders of the Epworth League, a Methodist youth organization which sought to enlist young people in fellowship, worship, study, and service. He was regarded as a member of the most liberal wing of the Methodist church, even tolerant of Roman Catholics and having friends among them.

When Father was a young child the family moved from Michigan to Southern California. It was there that he grew up while Grandfather served as pastor of several Methodist churches, meanwhile developing an interest in southwestern archaeology as an avocation. Gradually, the avocation replaced the ministerial profession, and for the last twenty years of his life Grandfather made a career of archaeological field work and lecturing. Thus, Father was introduced as a teen-ager to southwestern archaeology and assisted the pioneers in that area, Adolph F. A. Bandelier and others, in excavating such spectacular sites as Puje and Pajarito in New Mexico. These early experiences established his course toward a career in anthropology.

Father and Mother met while they were both students at Northwestern University. She too came from an ardent Methodist background; her ancestors had entertained the circuit riders and had built the first Methodist church in Plano, Illinois. During my childhood devout Methodism was much in evidence, complete with grace at meals, family prayer, and Bible reading before Sunday school. Father was liberal enough to let me change, in about the year of the Dayton trial, from a Methodist to a Baptist Sunday school which was attended by many of my friends and where I liked the teacher better. My home was an unlikely place to look for an "infidel" or "heretic" or for one of those who, as William Jennings Bryan described evolutionists during the trial, "shut God out of the world" and "take from little children their belief in a God. . . ."

Father graduated from college in 1903, did post-graduate work at Chicago and in Germany, and in 1906 accepted a position with the

Field Museum (now Chicago Natural History Museum), and set off for a honeymoon that was to last for six years mostly among the wild tribes of the Philippines. Returning to the States he earned his doctorate in anthropology from Columbia University.

In 1923, upon my parents' return from field work in Southeast Asia, the University of Chicago bid for Father's services and he spent 1924 there as a lecturer on anthropology before deciding to shift to Chicago permanently. He went as the one man to represent anthropology within the Department of Sociology. His office was literally a janitor's closet that had been cleaned out to make room for him. Classes were small and considerable improvisation was necessary to provide teaching materials. For example, I was regularly utilized as a specimen in evening laboratories where students of physical anthropology learned the techniques of measuring body dimensions on living subjects.

Then, down in Tennessee, John T. Scopes was arrested and indicted for teaching evolution in the public schools in violation of a state law that had gone into effect only six weeks earlier. The fundamentalists, led by William Jennings Bryan, saw this as a chance to dramatize their battle against evolution and their offer to participate in the prosecution of Scopes was quickly accepted.

Bryan had been battling evolution for some time. His book *In His Image* (1922) presents a prolonged attack on Darwin and his theories and formulates in advance some of the principal points that were to be used in the prosecution of Scopes; for example, "If it is contended that an instructor has a right to teach anything he likes, I reply that the parents who pay the salary have a right to decide what shall be taught." [1] Also in 1922 Bryan wrote:

The only part of evolution in which any considerable interest is felt is evolution applied to man. A hypothesis in regard to the rocks and plant life does not affect the philosophy upon which one's life is built. Evolution applied to fish, birds and beasts would not materially affect man's view of his own responsibilities except as the acceptance of an unsupported hypothesis as to these would be used to support a similar hypothesis as to man. The evolution that is harmful—distinctly so—is the evolution that destroys man's family tree as taught by the Bible and makes him a descendant of the lower forms of life. This, as I shall try to show, is a very vital matter. [2]

1 William Jennings Bryan, *In His Image* (New York: Fleming H. Revell, 1922), 122.
2 "God and Evolution," New York *Times* (February 26, 1922), Sec. 7, p. 1.

It is easy to see why, in 1925, a scientist prepared expressly to defend the evolution of man should be the special enemy of the followers of Bryan. Biologists and geologists could be relatively minor nuisances, to be deplored because of the danger that their conclusions on evolution might be generalized to man. Even theologians who could see no necessary conflict between religion and evolution and who considered that evolution might have been God's way of creating man were relatively tolerable. Bryan had written: "It is true that a God who could make man as he is, could have made him by the long drawn-out process suggested by Darwin. To do either would require infinite power, beyond the ability of man to comprehend." [3] But Bryan had declared Darwinism to be a demoralizing and corruptive influence. Clearly there was no room for his disciples to compromise with a scientist prepared to discuss the scientific evidence and defend the evolution of man from preexisting and nonhuman forms of life. And this was just the role into which my father was cast.

I do not know to what extent my father was acquainted with Clarence Darrow before he received the phone call from him, in which Darrow said, "Malone, Colby, and I don't know much about evolution. We don't know who to call as witnesses. But we are fighting your battle for academic freedom and we need the help of you fellows at the university." That afternoon, zoologist H. H. Newman, Dean of the Divinity School Shailer Mathews, and my father met with Darrow to plan the scientific defense. (Clarence Darrow was the only other principal of the trial whom I came to know to any extent. As a teen-ager I was invited to his home on various occasions, particularly when he had teen-aged relatives as house guests. During these visits I had the opportunity to hear him expound on some of his heterodox views and even to argue with him using all the erudition that teen-agers are capable of marshaling for such occasions. Darrow was at least an agnostic and, I think, a little beyond that, probably possessing some slight positive conviction of the nonexistence of God.)

Bryan was evidently caught by surprise by the attempt to introduce scientific testimony and the testimony of experts on the Scriptures. He even appealed, in what must have been desperation, to the Catholic University of America for a statement opposing evolution,

3. Bryan, *In His Image,* 110.

but was rebuffed by an answer that excited my father's lifelong admiration. I deeply regret that, despite intense efforts, I have been unable to locate a copy of this statement which emphasized that God created man but that evolution might have been His way. As a matter of fact, Bryan received remarkably little support from other religious groups, including other northern Protestants. This is probably attributable less to any enthusiasm for evolution among those groups than to concern over Bryan's efforts to have his own special brand of fundamentalism endorsed by law.

On Sunday, July 12, Bryan spoke to an overflow crowd at the Methodist Church, South in Dayton where he oratorically welcomed this chance for a "duel to the death with this slimy thing." But on Thursday, July 16, he devoted the time for his heralded "great speech" to a plea against the admission of expert testimony. He won on the legal point but, on Darrow's instructions, the expert witnesses prepared statements of the testimony they would have given and these were released to the press despite the objection of Judge Raulston that "they might reach the jury."

My father's affidavit (Appendix C), written at that time, could be a brief summary of an introductory anthropology course of the day. He attempted to explain why "evidence abundantly justifies us in believing that development has been from the simple to the complex and that present forms of life, including man, have been produced from earlier existing forms, but through immense periods of time."

He called attention to man's vestigial organs—structures such as the appendix and the muscles that move the ears which are useless to us but which serve important functions in other animals. He noted the one-to-one correspondence of bones and organs in man and in certain other animals. He stated that man and the anthropoid apes must have branched off of a common stock, in which case "we might hope to find in ancient strata of the rocks some evidences of earlier forms of men, who might perhaps more closely approach the common ancestor." Then he briefly reviewed the fossil evidence of men and "ape men."

As I compare that statement with the account of human evolution found in a leading college textbook of zoology published more than a quarter of a century later, I am impressed by the firm and definite conclusions that could be drawn in 1925 from the then scanty fossil evidence. Both the affidavit and the 1951 textbook give minor attention to the Piltdown find which has since been revealed as a hoax.

Pithecanthropus, the "Java man," had been found in 1891 and the affidavit correctly describes its status as a primitive human. But it was impossible to make a detailed statement in 1925 or to foresee such developments as potassium-argon dating which has now established the age of this find at 600,000 years. The first of some forty Chinese Pithecanthropus ("Peking man") was found in 1927, and the next find in Java was made in 1935. With their newer evidence anthropologists today can state firmly that Pithecanthropus had limb bones indistinguishable from those of modern man but that his skull had many primitive apelike features and housed a brain that is small by modern standards. Nevertheless, he made crude stone tools and used fire. Father's affidavit refers to Raymond Dart's discovery in Africa "a few months ago" of another primitive "ape-man," but it was to be another twenty-five years before additional finds would prove that Australopithecus was really a man rather than an ape.

In 1925 the biochemical evidence for the kinship of apes and man was scanty and had not been integrated into the field of anthropology; consequently it is not mentioned in the affidavit. It is this biochemical similarity that makes monkeys and apes susceptible to many of the same diseases and parasites as man—much to the distress of zoo keepers and the delight of medical researchers. This similarity also makes the primates, including man, nearly unique among animals in requiring vitamin C in the diet, no doubt because our remote common ancestors lost the ability to synthesize ascorbic acid in the body. The blood groups of the AB system had been discovered in 1900 but their inheritance was still poorly understood in 1925 and it was not clear that they represented specific proteins that can often be useful in tracing paternity and other relationships. Would Bryan have been impressed if he could have been told that the anthropoid apes have the same AB blood groups that occur in man, that the "Rh factor" which has received so much publicity as a cause of death in newborn human infants received its name from the fact that it was first discovered in rhesus monkeys?

The precipitin test, which measures the similarity of proteins from different animals, was used as early as 1904 by George Nuttall for judging relationships among various animals but conclusive evidence of man's relationships had not yet been obtained by this technique in 1925. For this test some animal, usually a rabbit, is immunized by injections of human blood serum which cause it to develop antibodies against human proteins. If serum from the rabbit is then mixed with human serum a heavy precipitate will form, whereas very little precipitate will result from mixing the rabbit serum with that of an animal distantly related to man, say a fish or a bird. This test shows that human serum and chimpanzee serum have more proteins in common than either has with monkey serum. But the chimpanzee, man, and monkey serums have more in common than any of them has with the serum of any nonprimate. Thus the fundamental chemistry of living things is, with every increase in our knowledge, supporting the evolutionary relationships of man as they were known to anthropologists forty years ago.

This knowledge of man's relations is of the utmost importance for some of the most progressive fields of current medical research. I cannot help thinking of the mischief that Bryan would have committed if the fundamentalist views had prevailed over the scientific evidence then available and if scientists had therefore stopped teaching and working on the assumption that the primates are more closely related to man than are other animals. Without this knowledge of biochemical affinity no one would have attempted to conquer polio by growing the virus on the kidneys of monkeys.

It is of the utmost importance that our new generations of research workers understand these evolutionary relationships in all the detail available. For example, consider the hormones, those complex chemical regulators of many of our body functions. The antidiabetic hormone, insulin, was first prepared by Sir Frederick Grant Banting and his associates in 1922. It was found that insulin could be obtained from the stockyards because the insulin of cattle, sheep, and pigs was effective in controlling human diabetes. A few years later the growth-controlling hormone of the pituitary gland was discovered and it was natural to assume that pituitary hormone from the stockyards could be used to correct the deficiency in human dwarfs. This, however, was not the case and it was only when large numbers of rhesus monkeys were shipped to the United States for the preparation of Salk polio vaccine that enough monkey pituitary hormone became available for tests that showed that it *is* effective in humans. The day may conceivably come when colonies of chimpanzees or gorillas will save uncounted human lives. Today there is an active field of research concerned with the problems of transplanting tissues and organs between individuals and between species. In 1965 it is impossible to say how important such studies will ultimately be but nothing is more certain than that they could not even have been conceived if the teaching of human evolution had been halted forty years ago.

The fact of evolution, and even some of the details of the process, are now so thoroughly understood that they are the starting points for today's theoretical biology.

We are actually learning to read the genetic code that constitutes the "information" passed from one generation to the next, telling the fertilized egg how to go about developing. Just as magnetic impulses on a tape coated with iron oxide instruct a tape-player so that a Beethoven symphony emerges from the speaker, so a sequence of organic bases on a long tapelike molecule of "DNA" (deoxyribonucleic acid) instructs the egg on what to do next with the result that an orderly embryonic development, far more complex than any symphony conceived by man, emerges. DNA was discovered just before the beginning of the twentieth century but it was not until 1928, when bacteria of one genetic strain were transformed into another strain by adding DNA from the second strain, that there was a hint that this compound was indeed the all important genetic link between generations. And it took us another twenty years to be sure of this fact. Today we are learning about evolution at this fundamental level. We know, for example, that the change of one "letter" (organic base) in the DNA "message" gives to certain human populations in Africa a resistance to malaria that makes them more fit in their native environment than others would be.

Evolution, directed by Darwinian natural selection, has won the controversy. We are now seeing evolution occurring on a wholesale scale as bacteria evolve resistance to one antibiotic after another and as insects similarly evolve resistance to a succession of new insecticides. How helpless we should be when confronted with these developments if we lacked such understanding as we have of the evolutionary processes! Furthermore we have learned to read enough of the genetic code to confirm that the code of the anthropoid apes is composed in a language more like that of man than of other animals. This is a fantastically great advance over what was known in 1925 but we can be grateful that enough was known then to ward off what would have amounted to a legal imposition of ignorance.

All indications today are that the next forty years will yield a much greater increase in our knowledge of biological processes than has occurred since the Dayton trial. We now contemplate the impending exploration of other planets. Nothing excites the biologist more than some of the evolutionary questions that may be answered by such explorations. Is there only one way in which evolution could have proceeded or was the course that it followed on earth an accident? There are some peculiar chemical similarities among all of the organisms on earth that provide the potentiality for answering this question if we can obtain organisms from other planets to compare with them.

The molecules of sugars and many other organic compounds are asymmetrical and their particular type of asymmetry is easily determined in the laboratory from the direction in which they rotate a beam of polarized light passing through them. Now, it is a very curious thing that almost all of the sugars that occur in living things on earth are "right-handed" and rotate the plane of a beam of polarized light in the sense of a screw with a right-hand thread. At the same time, virtually all of the natural amino acids, of which the proteins, the principal building blocks of our bodies, are composed, are left-handed. But when we synthesize such compounds in the laboratory we typically obtain mixtures with about 50 percent of the molecules being the mirror images of those found in nature.

We have no reason to think that the mirror images of these molecules should not be equally suitable as building blocks for living organisms. Will we find organisms on Mars with some of the symmetries reversed? If so, we shall probably conclude that all present day organisms on earth have inherited the ability to use asymmetrical molecules of one configuration from the first organisms on earth which, by chance, started with that configuration. If, on the other hand, there are living things on other planets with the same biochemical peculiarities as earthly organisms, we must wonder if they had a common origin with us or if there is some fundamental law of asymmetry that makes other forms of life impossible. Such questions are among the most fundamental and exciting of the twentieth century. But if Bryan and his colleagues had prevailed forty years ago we should not be asking such questions now. Students in the United States would be receiving an education more appropriate for the sixteenth century than for the present.

What did the trial of John T. Scopes accomplish? As a legal spectacle the trial did little to inspire confidence in our judicial system. The jury heard only a few minutes of the trial and none of the testimony. The defense witnesses were not even allowed to testify. The proceedings were designed to provide the basis for an appeal to a higher court, but even that was not to be because of the technicality that the judge had no legal right to invoke a fine of over $50 without advice of the jury. And the classic exchanges between Bryan and Darrow were expunged from the record. It is tempting to conclude, as did my father, that "Tennessee had been made to appear so ridiculous in the eyes of the nation that other states did not care to follow its lead." [4] Scopes and other contributors to the present volume are in essential agreement with this conclusion and I certainly am not qualified to disagree. But, if the trial did indeed inhibit other states, it is really frightening to consider what might have happened without it.

In October, 1925, the Texas State Textbook Board ordered deletion of all references to evolution in books for the public schools. In February, 1926, the governor of Mississippi signed an anti-evolution bill into law. Within two years of the trial anti-evolution bills were also introduced in Arkansas, California, Florida, Maine, Missouri, New Hampshire, North Dakota, Oklahoma, and West Virginia. These bills failed except in Arkansas where the electorate passed the law on election day, November 7, 1928. The Arkansas voters could not have been much impressed with the "ridiculous" image of Tennessee, for the first act under the new law, executed within a week of passage, was to ban Webster's dictionary from all public schools, including the state university, because it described evolution as supported by scientific facts!

It is no doubt true that where, before Scopes's trial, one person had read about evolution, ten did so afterwards. It is also tempting to conclude that this increased public awareness would dispel ignorance. How much should we be concerned by isolated bits of evidence to the contrary? Quite recently the California State Superintendent of Public Instruction recommended that textbooks be edited to meet the objections of anti-evolutionists. The state board of education, in this allegedly progressive state, overruled him only on January 9, 1964!

As for the impact of the trial on my father, he returned to Chicago to learn from university officials that demands for his

4 *Scientific American*, CC (January, 1959), 120–30.

dismissal already exceeded those that had ever before been received for a faculty member. In the autumn he innocently went to give the first lecture in Introductory Anthropology and found a room so packed that it violated city fire ordinances. He thought that perhaps he was in the wrong room and asked a student what course was meeting. The reply was: "Anthropology. The prof who teaches it defended that fellow Scopes." From that time on Introductory Anthropology required a large lecture hall each year. By 1929 Father was chairman of a growing Department of Anthropology, newly separated from sociology. It is my understanding that today the University of Chicago remains preeminent in anthropology and that the department is still growing. Certainly, former students who received their training there are very much in evidence in other departments of anthropology around the world. And some inestimable part of the initial impetus for all this must be attributed to a 1925 court trial in Dayton, Tennessee.

PART FIVE

THE THEOLOGIANS

This living creature, Adam, is placed by God in a garden, which he is to till. He is forbidden to eat of the tree of knowledge of good and evil. He, however, disobeys and eats the fruit. God then declares that man has become "one of us knowing good and evil." Genesis thus says that an animal life, produced by God from the earth by His spirit, came to be like God through a development born of experience. Thus so far from opposing the Genesis account of the creation of man, the theory of evolution in some degree resembles it.

SHAILER F. MATHEWS
July 20, 1925

THEOLOGY IN CONFLICT

JOHN DILLENBERGER

J OHN DILLENBERGER, a graduate of Union Theological
Seminary, received his Ph.D. from Columbia University. Or-
dained in the United Church of Christ in 1943, he served as a U.S.
Navy chaplain for the next three years. He has taught theology at
Union Theological Seminary, Harvard Divinity School, and Prince-
ton, Columbia, and Drew Universities, and is presently Dean and
Professor of Historical Theology, Graduate Theological Union,
Berkeley. His most recent book is concerned with Protestant thought
and the natural sciences.

My agreement to comment on the Scopes trial is based on a continued interest in the relations between theology and science. But
aside from this theoretical interest, I, too, confess to some personal
association with the Scopes trial.

The event might have escaped my attention had it not been for the
delight of an uncle who relished the contest between William Jennings Bryan and Clarence Darrow as one between two boxing
champions. Indeed he defined the trial in such terms and seemed
more interested in the contest itself than in the results. Thus my early
association with the trial had the stamp of neutrality. I also associated with it the fanfare of a major athletic contest, for my earliest
recollection of newspaper headlines are of stories of this trial. The
drama in the trial is certainly evident from the fact that of the

events of the twenties I recall the Scopes trial, the Lindbergh flight, and the beginning of the Great Depression.

Perhaps because I was too young, the issues did not seem important. In fact, in that southern Illinois region, where North and South intersected, I have no recollection that the issues were felt deeply or clearly articulated. But, there is no doubt about the national significance of the event. Those interested could be said to reflect three camps: first, the group which passionately held to the literal truth of Scripture, that is, the whole fundamentalist bloc; second, those who were fiercely interested in attacking this approach; and finally, those for whom the issues were not burning, who, if they had not themselves solved the problem, at least had pushed it far to the side with a feeling that it was not central, or who in some sense had already come to terms with the issues now again being debated. The latter had all the characteristics of spectators in the best sense of the term.

In any historical framework, the trial was at the end of an era rather than at the beginning. Countless people had come to terms with the issue of evolution, but in retrospect, the alternatives of the period may have left much to be desired. Perhaps the inadequacy of these answers more than anything else account for the seriousness and curiosity which mingled to provide the dramatic context for the trial. Of course, there was an attempt to put Dayton, Tennessee, upon the map, and the known gambits of the time were employed. Indeed, there was an issue of civil liberties, but such issues hardly draw that kind of rapt attention. There was the drama of national figures, William Jennings Bryan and Clarence Darrow in particular, but neither would qualify as a perceptive thinker for either position. Their reputation and competence lay in other areas, and here both were exposed beyond their depth of learning.

In an age of normalcy when no great issues were pushing for attention, the trial became important. During times of duress and crisis it might well have been sidetracked. In short, the particular ingredients in the social setting provided the possibility for attention upon the trial. But the ethos for this catalyst was the uneasy acceptance of long-standing answers, irrespective of which side propounded them.

This is not the time or place to go into the history of evolution and evolutionary thought, but certain widely accepted judgments may be repeated as background material. In the first instance, the notion of evolution was a philosophical concept, coming to clearest expression in modern time during the first half of the nineteenth century. It was rather reluctantly and belatedly accepted among scientists, indeed, only when the painstaking evidence of Darwin and his associates demanded it. The wedding of a powerful philosophical idea and its apparent corroboration in nature were all the ingredients necessary for providing a total understanding of life. Historical memory and conditioning were full of the amalgam of theology, philosophy, and science. The particular Protestant and Roman Catholic syntheses might have been abandoned, but the notion of a synthesis was still strongly felt, no matter under whose aegis, as long as it provided total and full explanations, sometimes demanding and sometimes excluding God. It was inevitable, therefore, that this new theory should now be applied with a vengeance to all that was under the sun, even including the sun itself.

Time has had a winnowing effect upon the evolutionary hypothesis. Just as in the case of the Copernican theory, the basic scientific notion, however much it has had to be modified, has survived, whereas the philosophical accompaniments have been largely abandoned. Obviously, the notion of development remains. Such development has certainly proved to be more complicated and less single-directed than the earlier proponents of the evolutionary theories surmised. Moreover, it is apparent that the notion of development does not carry its own interpretation, but is itself subject to diverse interpretations.

In any historical understanding of what happened, it is important to note that it was exceedingly difficult for a contemporary of the time to distinguish the scientific aspects from the philosophical encasements. Indeed, this has been true in virtually every significant scientific advance until the modern era, when scientists have, by and large for this reason, deliberately eschewed a philosophical orientation. It was largely the inability to cut this knot which led many to solutions about which they were uneasy unless they shared the assumptions of one of the two major divergent parties. It was easier generally for the fundamentalist and for the person who accepted the evolutionary hypothesis as valid in all areas of human existence. But it is apparent that these alternatives were not feasible and that the respective gradations in between were compromises rather than directions in which the problem might have received new formulations.

Let us look briefly at the alternatives. On the one side was the entire fundamentalist heritage, the product of an orthodoxy which had lost its intellectual finesse. Protestant orthodoxy had been a monumental creation of the expression of faith, even though it confused the articulation of truth with faith itself. In the earlier Augustinian tradition, faith had been an illuminating center for encompassing all of the pieces of human knowledge. But Protestant orthodoxy had functioned as an ordering movement, classifying, elaborating, and arranging all knowledge in a total system of truth. Essentially, it collected information, unified all aspects, and provided a stable picture. It had little feeling for the evolving of truth or for new discoveries that did not fit traditional patterns. When, therefore, new discoveries occurred outside the long-accepted consistencies, such knowledge could only be considered in error. The subsequent inability to use faith creatively in a time of intellectual crisis for the elaboration of new formulations led orthodoxy to atrophy, that is, to produce the unreflective and repetitive stress on inherited truth, particularly the literal truth of Scripture. The reduced range of the fundamentalist concern, now emphasizing Scripture as the sole criterion of knowledge, was itself the sign that the former stress on the significance of all areas of knowledge had been abandoned. Now Scripture alone remained as the deposit of knowledge rather than as the medium of faith.

Since fundamentalism abandoned the passion for the unification of knowledge and insisted on Scripture as the central norm of truth, fundamentalism had few first-rate thinkers. Two exceptional figures were Charles Hodge, the most influential professor at Princeton Theological Seminary in its early classical period, and J. Gresham Machen, the great conservative New Testament scholar; they reflected the older wedding of knowledge and Scripture. For the most part, however, fundamentalism exhibited an uncritical insistence upon Scripture as literal knowledge. It was the residue of a legacy in which theological explication was knowledge of all things. Fundamentalism, in which Scripture is simply a book of knowledge, is consequently vestigial. Historical sediments of this type are defended more by passion than by insight, and William Jennings Bryan was Exhibit A.

The fundamentalist reaction was certainly related to the only alternatives which it could envisage. It may be difficult to determine which is cause and which is consequence, and the decision for one or the other side may in fact reflect the stance from which one is viewing the problem. But it is important to note that Protestant orthodox and fundamentalist defenders alike could not see any genuine Christian substance in the understanding of their mutual opponents and found themselves arguing that capitulation at one point meant capitulation all along the line. The latter alternative was certainly real at some junctures, but the question is whether it was universally or necessarily true.

Darwin had admitted that his sensibilities for other areas of inquiry and affirmation than that of science had been considerably dulled by his own preoccupations. Huxley had made both a theology and a philosophy out of evolution while shying away from traditional theology. It was questionable whether any of the alternatives to orthodoxy remotely represented either the misery and grandeur of man as conceived biblically or other traditions of philosophical understanding in the West. The question, therefore, was never one of science versus religion, but of philosophical origins and ingredients. It was undoubtedly for this reason that the conservative Charles Hodge, who had managed to come to terms with the new astronomy, could not accept what Darwinism did to the main ingredient in the God-man relation, namely, man himself.

For the conservatives, the situation was not alleviated but rather was aggravated by those who made a positive Christian conception out of Darwinism. Two examples may be mentioned. Henry Drummond—a scientific and lay theologian, a man of considerable piety and a thorough student of Scripture—stressed not the origin of man, but man's destiny, what might happen to him in the transformation of his existence in the light of the gospel. He turned evolution into a positive direction. Lyman Abbott, a popular and disciplined liberal theologian, believed evolution and progress in social terms were virtually identical. In Jesus of Nazareth particularly, all the possibilities in nature and history had been made articulate and normative for man. Indeed, in Drummond and Abbott evolution and progress in individual and social terms had been joined together.

The issue was certainly not the right of any individuals to hold such positions, but the chasm between the fundamentalist and the liberal Protestant versions. One could ask whether the progressive, evolutionary, philosophical outlook—which the events of history were subsequently to call into question—was definitionally Christian (which should be distinguished from the traditional question whether or not a *person* is a Christian) or whether it represented an independent position for which support was wrested from the traditional Christian materials. Those who were caught up in the evolutionary religious position faced no uncomfortable problem. On every side, it appeared as if the evidence of personal and social history was giving substance to their dreams. At the same time, they had discovered a new religious freedom opposed to the traditional oppressive demands of doctrine, tradition, and ethos. Fundamentalists, too, had the virtue of a clear and simple position, although they were uncomfortable because the error of the opposing forces ought not really to be permitted, though they had themselves accepted living in a land of freedom of expression. Those who could accept neither the obscurantism of fundamentalism nor the progressivism of the evolutionary conception had no genuine place to go nor an articulate alternative. They were quietly uneasy, keeping more of the Christian substance than the evolutionists but accepting the scientific aspect of the evolutionary hypothesis. Theirs was an opportunity for which history gave no clear and articulate voice. It is because of them that the smoldering problems could always be fanned into a burning fire.

In reading the statement by W. C. Curtis in this volume, it seems to me to be quite apparent that he belongs to those for whom evolution is fact and philosophy and theology. The insistence upon openness on the part of the fundamentalist against their demand for concrete statements about the origin of species is admirable; but it is undermined at the same time by the apparent assumption that scientists alone face the facts and that evolution is the only reasonable explanation. Evolution as a descriptive statement covering various developments is not at issue here. But what is at issue is the inability to distinguish such descriptions from a more comprehensive and total statement. It is not sufficiently recognized by Curtis, as by others, that the plea for openness, which evolutionists demanded, carried within itself a certain restrictiveness which denied openness to those who were not necessarily fundamentalists. For example, Dr. Curtis confesses to a certain agnostic position, but this does not keep him from making theological judgments: "It is more reasonable to believe that the Bible is a human document representing the history of an advance from the concept of a barbarous and revengeful Jehovah of the earlier Old Testament, to the God of Righteouness and Justice of the later prophets, and culminating in the concept of the Father as preached by Jesus of Nazareth." [1] This was a widely held position at one time. But more recent scholarship has convincingly demonstrated that it is a position which was more brought to the materials than actually taken from them.

Kirtley F. Mather, the only contributor to this book who has been my friend and colleague, is infinitely more careful in his distinctions than Dr. Curtis. He does not confuse evolution in the scientific sense with evolution as a philosophic and theological concept. As a consequence, he is more careful both in his delineation of evolution and of religious factors. Fundamentally it appears that his position is one of seeing analogies between the two domains of knowledge—analogies which may even lead to mutual support while maintaining the fundamental difference. As there is evolution in the scientific fields, so there is evolution also in the religious sensibilities of man. But the former is not necessarily the basis of the latter. Indeed Mather's conception of analogy is reminiscent of that propounded earlier by Drummond. Mather even talks of scientific and of spiritual fields. He is apparently convinced that there is a material realm and a spiritual realm, independent but correlative or analagous. Again, this need not be denied, but it is a question of historical interest whether such a position is at all related to what has been accepted as the main contours of classical Christian heritage. Both Dr. Curtis and Dr. Mather seem somehow aware of this, for they find it necessary to repudiate, not to reinterpret, traditional Christian theology.

Like myself, LaMont C. Cole is not directly involved in the Scopes trial, except by the fact of birth. Insofar as his paper goes, it seems to me that he is concerned only with the idea that scientific evidence generally supports evolution in the scientific sense. Although a definite facility of theory is evident, this still leaves open whatever additional views he may have. One might desire more, but is grateful for the openness which is evident in Dr. Cole's paper.

It is here that we enter into the new situation which does make the Scopes trial look drastically different forty years after. Theologically, we have come a long way. We no longer find it necessary to reject the theology of the past. Instead, we try to interpret its inner meaning, dynamics, or intentionality. Rather than drawing insights from Scripture or accepting it literally, we have learned to

1 See Appendix A.

sense a biblical normativeness without inhibiting imagination or evidence.

We already live in a post-neoorthodox age, that age which retains the classical theological position rather than the liberal while maintaining the critical and historical concerns of the writer. The neoorthodox movement, dramatically hitting the American theological scene a decade after the Scopes trial, was responsible for new alternatives and perspectives on the evolutionary issue. Neoorthodoxy was never fundamentalist in its outlook upon Scripture, although the extreme liberals had difficulty in understanding that this was the case. Nor was it modernistic in its imaginative use of Scripture, though the fundamentalists never understood that this was the case. Neoorthodoxy, like all movements of protest and affirmation, overemphasized various aspects; but that is inevitable in history. Those who look for balance are seldom happy with historical developments.

Basic to the neoorthodox affirmation was the contention that a living God was quite different from the domesticated God of the evolutionary theists, that He instead confronted man simultaneously in judgment and mercy. More accurately it could be said that the mercy of God was considered to be both the source of judgment and of redemptive concern. In the early stages of the movement the stress lay upon the sovereign judgment and upon man's sinful rebellion. These obviously stood against the man of progress and the God of familiarity and stressed that the relation of the living God to the living man was quite different than the evolutionary theories had indicated. Indeed, the difference between these two theological positions was as vast as the notion of the wholly other God seemed to imply.

Since the concern in the neoorthodox development was with God and man and with the crisis and hope of man before God, it centered upon history as the matrix for theological understanding. The problems of the cosmos and of origin were significantly and deliberately sidetracked. The exodus—that is, the miraculously experienced deliverance from Egypt as the clue to historical understanding and therefore to God's creative activity—became more important than the concrete facts of history or the concrete questions of origin and of creation in themselves. God is the Lord of History. As the God who is Redeemer and Creator, He is the God before whom the particular questions of origin and the evolutionary scheme seem irrelevant. Indeed neoorthodoxy did not concern itself with these problems of origin. And existentialism, with its concern only for those issues which directly and experientially affect one's existence, bracketed out such issues. They are considered questions with which man may deal but they are not significant theologically. Evolution as a scientific category is neither denied nor affirmed; it is accepted as such but considered peripheral to the theological concerns. Such an attitude stands in rather stark contrast to the issues of the Scopes trial, and this fact in itself indicates something of the transformation of the entire theological spectrum since 1925.

While we live in a post-neoorthodox age, all of the subjects and alternatives are dependent upon its basic reconception of the theological task. At some levels, existentialist and neoorthodox theologies may be diametrically opposite. But with respect to the particular issue at hand, existentialism, with its passion to conceptualize only that which is encountered in existence, is the programmatic attempt to narrow all of the problems of theology to those of the God-man relation and, in this sense, theology can be said to be anthropology. In this respect existentialism falls within the rubrics of liberal theology, but its program is dramatically different. The program of demythologizing does not intend to abandon the biblical issues but rather to interpret them properly for our ears. There is a passion in existentialism for the biblical message and an adherence to its basic intentions which removes it from the earlier problems of liberalism where evolution and the concerns of Jesus of Nazareth were identified. Even the concern with Jesus as the instance of faith in the contemporary hermeneutical discussion couches the question in the biblical orbit in contrast to the general cultural setting out of which the previous discussions emerged.

Hence, in contemporary theological discussions, the problems of science and faith as they emerged in the Scopes trial no longer are a matter of concern. They have been bracketed out or abandoned. There is a kind of division between the realms of science and the realms of theology, a division which it has been necessary to establish for the sake of the possibility of seeing new analogies. Such analogies are being built afresh by such individuals who have some competence in science and in theology as Harold Schilling, physicist and Dean of the Graduate School, Pennsylvania State University, and Ian Barbour, professor of physics and religion at Carleton College, Northfield, Minnesota. In them both the promise and peril of such enterprises become apparent. We have learned to be more careful than our predecessors and therefore the distinctions between realms are more important for us. But we cannot live in a split world. Faith demands of us that we accept its fragmentedness with a vision of the whole, being careful not to attempt to put things together too easily nor prematurely.

We are entering a theological period in which the various facets of knowledge will be related to each other and in which theology has again recovered its own integrity. With that new-won freedom, theology will again attempt to relate itself to all the areas of knowledge, as they in turn are being related to each other. On that path, all have a new wariness and take greater care. We shall not escape mistakes but, in faith, we can risk those too.

The period into which we are moving is one in which the conflicts of the Scopes trial are behind us, and such conflicts will probably not emerge again as matters of major import. But concurrently we shall probably abandon the isolation or rigid separation between the concerns of science and of theology. We shall try again with new courage and with the realization that we are also justified by faith in matters of the intellect. Therefore, we shall use our minds to the utmost, knowing the fragmentary character of all the formulations of theological work. Our time finds the alternatives of the Scopes trial quite unsatisfactory and has moved into directions which are quite different in perspective. The Scopes trial, while dramatic and significant, is nevertheless a back eddy in a stream which is moving clearly in quite different directions.

DAYTON'S LONG HOT SUMMER

CARLYLE MARNEY

CARLYLE MARNEY, a native of Tennessee, did his undergraduate work at Carson-Newman College and Southern Baptist Theological Seminary; he received his Th.D. from the latter in 1948. He has served pastorates in Kentucky and Texas and is now the senior minister of Myers Park Baptist Church, Charlotte, North Carolina. Although identified with a religious denomination that tends to be fundamentalist, Marney's writings and theological position are in contrast to and a criticism of this background.

When word reached the Ohio Dayton that two of her sons had actually gotten their plane off the ground at Kitty Hawk, the town unbeliever is reliably reported to have said: "That's not so. Nobody can fly; nobody ever did; nobody ever will; and if they did, they wouldn't be anybody from Dayton, Ohio!" We had our skeptical ones, too, in East Tennessee that long hot summer of 1925. They knew fundamentalism and they knew Dayton, Tennessee—furthermore, they knew that fundamentalism wasn't dying; it never did die, it never would die, and if it did die it wouldn't do it in Dayton, Tennessee. It couldn't get killed from there. But the more timidly belief-ful of us felt that something big was coming off just across the mountain on another tributary of the Tennessee and at twilight we watched for the lights of Armageddon. The Lord himself, some said, who was not too great to begin in Nazareth, would wind up

his business with all skeptics in little Dayton. Everybody who
mattered had already come in on the Southern from New York or
the C.N.O. & T.P. from Chicago, except the Lord who would use
other transport; but his chief representative, the Great Commoner,
was already there, eating and drinking (iced tea) with Rhea
countians and other sinners. Indeed the word of his great enjoyment
of Dayton victuals already qualified him as like his Lord in part (a
glutton, though no wine bibber).

Across forty years I remember the confusion with which all this
eschatalogical surging burst on a little fellow just making his way
from the "funny papers" to the front page of the Knoxville *Sentinel*.
It was my first big news interest and horribly upsetting. It seems
that some Yankees from New York had infiltrated with a high school
teacher named Darwin or Darrow or some name like that and he had
been teaching some very bad stuff about science that was against God
and good and white folks and this was very bad. In the *Sentinel* you
straighten this out. The teacher is not Charles Darwin—he is a
lawyer who thinks a book a fellow named Darrow wrote is all right
and Mr. Bryan ought to like it too. But hearing your elders talk it
all comes clear at last:

Charles Darwin isn't even at the trial, they tell you. He's dead
already; and besides, the schoolteacher isn't Darrow; it's just a boy
from Paducah and the university at Lexington by the name of
Scopes. The fellow to watch is the slick city lawyer Mr. Darrow. You
see his picture in the paper; he's chewing a straw and looks a little
like a rougher John Barrymore you have been sneaking off to
watch on Saturday afternoons, but really he is more like the woodcut
of the Devil in a book called *Faust* you have thumbed through. But
you must not worry, the preacher says. Everything is going to turn
out right for Jesus. A great dragon-killer named Bryan has been
sent by God Almighty to rescue your Bible, home, church, and sanity.

Meanwhile you've been reading your granddad's Cincinnati *Post*
and here you begin to discover for yourself that the great white
knight has been made to look a fool by Darwin-Darrow, the dragon.
You decide that the knight is saying things he cannot prove and that
may not matter. Because most everybody keeps acting as if the
knight had been abused you secretly pull for the dragon.

Then, one day, the knight goes back to the lodge, eats his usual
mammoth dinner, drinks (some said) nearly a gallon of ice water,
and the Lord "took him home" right from the middle of his nap.

You begin to be sure that he was not a knight at all, but was really more like the Don Quixote in your book who fought a windmill he did not understand. You resolve to understand this dragon business and the summer is over, but across forty years you wonder if the crisis of confusion into which it threw you and the inquiry you started as an eight-year-old are not the only good things you know to have come out of Dayton that long ago boyhood summer.

I

It is good to remember trials like this. "Thoughts that hearts once broke for, we breathe cheaply in the common air." (Lowell) Other trials, too, have focused on comparatively obscure people as representative of a wrong or decadent pattern. Mr. Scopes has been more favored than most defendants in such trials. Jesus and Dreyfus and Dred Scott, who finished out his "free" life as a porter in a St. Louis hotel as much a slave as ever, I guess, did not do so well. Mr. Scopes, who saw the trial as a fantastic misdirection of what his hopes had called for, has been permitted a long and useful anonymity in his praiseworthy execution of the work his personal gifts made possible and his heritage demanded. There was no rancour nor vice in him that I can find and the trial that bears his name bears no contribution of his that adds to the mean and base display that came to Dayton. For him, and for me, it was a summer's incident to be forgotten—six years later when at age fourteen I began to play against the teams of Rhea County High School I did not even remember that this was where Scopes had taught and coached. And John Scopes, then (1931) in a third year of graduate studies at Chicago, had already (1929) helped map the oil resources of a great continent. It was much later that subterranean forces created in me by this exposure came back to the surface to explain my twenty-year pilgrimage toward a more nearly legitimate faith.

And yet, across forty years, I can still find myself resenting what was done to my beloved East Tennessee by a press just learning how to really handle "big" stories like the Floyd Collins cave story, the Lindbergh flight, and the "Monkey Trial." I disliked then and I despise now that dreadful ditty everybody sang:

> You can't make a monkey out of me
> Just because I came from Tennessee
> I refuse to think
> That I'm the missing link

I ain't got no monkey manners
Gee, I hate bananas, ...

But mostly we despised that "writing fellow" from Baltimore, H. L.
Mencken.

It's too late to quarrel with Mr. Mencken. He is dead and has no
real successor and besides I've come to read him with much enjoyment. Nor can the image he largely created from the facets of a
decadence he wished to see be corrected from here. The national
image of the South is seamed and serrated with concepts the language
of which he brilliantly minted. The only point to be sustained here
is that he saw what he came to see. It was (and is) there. Dayton's
summer did not kill it off. But there was more. Happily enough,
there were other influences than those seen by Mencken in East
Tennessee of 1925.

It is true that on summer nights we could hear on soft breezes
the shouting meetings of one of the sects in the red church building
with no floor at the foot of our long hill, but I was reading one or
another of the thousand books I borrowed in boyhood from the
splendid Andrew Carnegie Library at the other base of the same
hill. And likely we had already been to the Chautauqua Series for
which our mother had saved ticket money from somewhere. We had
heard Elihu Root on the tariff system, or some senator, or Ruth
Bryan Owen (handsome enough to attract great attention the
summer Aimee Semple McPherson was kidnaped[?]). Or we had
seen a Shakespearean touring company, or heard Bhomer Kriel's
great band, or a symphony. Within an eight-block area in a little
town of 3,500 souls not thirty minutes from Dayton, I can now recall
graduates of Harvard College (we had, it is said, the only man who
ever took a degree at Harvard without making a speaking acquaint-
ance), Yale University, the University of Tennessee, of Kentucky, of
Alabama, Georgia Tech, the Cincinnati Conservatory, Cornell. A
representative of Canadian culture at its best lived across the street
and supervised twelve million acres of forest. (I rode with him as a
boy, visited Sergeant York's parents, and wrote to Cornell to get a
catalogue in forestry). There were products of Louisville's best
society. My neighbor had retired from a distinguished Philadelphia
pastorate to serve the Presbyterian (Northern) church. The professor
of economics at the University of Tennessee was pastor of the
Christian Church. There was a lot of Yankee commercial connections

with timber, coal, iron; there was a Revolutionary War heritage; there were some devoted Roman Catholics, two splendid Jewish families; there was Boy's Week and Boy Scouts, photography, music, water sports, and all kinds of visiting pretty girls from Chattanooga. All in all, there was in East Tennessee a fantastic pluralism the reporters all missed. There was capital from New York (the East Tennessee Land Company had still nearly a half-million acres); there were industrial families from the North and Midwest (Dames, Flanders, Rockwells, Cassells). There were remnants of the social experiments of sons of British royalty who took up 100,000 acres and left behind their little libraries (with first editions of Darwin, *et al.*), their Anglican missions, and tennis. There were the New England cults (the Universalists had a temple of grand proportions—a la General Grant architecture—a block away), and temperance societies and social projects, and Harvard's silent graduate just four doors away. These all had their weight on us. And mostly it's still there. We knew Dayton's summer was a put-up job and that nothing really evil would die or live there too long.

II

What, then, was Dayton's summer? It was both more and less. It was much more than I knew then and probably much less than its modern appraisers have said. When Gunnar Myrdal calls the Dayton trial "the most spectacular manipulation of the general power of the fundamentalist clergy," [1] I am pressed now to ask— power to do what? Power, then, to threaten school boards, keep small schools from becoming universities, and generally create a din in the ears of small-town legislators. But even where the fundamentalists had majority status they changed no single social situation for the better and the people who walked in darkness have still seen no great light. Provincialism wears a thousand kinds of dress in its thousand settings. Occasionally some village becomes a stage for a drama which reveals the "tragic, laggard back-log of immovables" in so bright a light as to sear eyeballs and brand a region for decades. This, at least, happened in Dayton where what was underneath a real estate scheme became a tragicomic Vanity Fair; but provincialism is everywhere. For even the quote I used to set up the drama of "tragic laggard" backlogs is from the provincial Thomas

1 Gunnar Myrdal, *An American Dilemma* (New York: Harper and Brothers, 1944), 458.

Carlyle who called Darwin the "apostle of dirt worship with the
petulance natural to a dyspeptic eunuch."

A Vanity Fair indeed, for most of Dayton's crowds were imported. While there was enough "truth" in the reportage to make
the press treatment of Tennessee no real slander, the color was not
nearly all a local brand. It came in from everywhere. Forty years
later Tennessee still has its provincialism. But the East Tennessean
is a breed apart and he does well when transplanted and sometimes
he does well at Oak Ridge, for example, where the mountain at last
came to Mahomet. At heart he is *turista*, too, at a Vanity Fair not
his home. Dayton was an orgy for the entrepreneurs of a "managed
Credulity," to use Arthur Murphy's fine phrase, but it was also
more than this.

Upon an issue settled for most thinkers nearly a half-century
before, the Dayton trial became a seizure, a paroxysm, a grand colic
in the bowel of the American folk-religion. It was not matched in
bitterness between the trials of the accused accomplices in assassi-
nation of Mr. Lincoln and the Joe McCarthy hearings in Washington, nearly ninety years apart. It comes between these trials and
represents, to use another anatomical figure, the lancing of a boil.
There drained off the poison of dying old flesh which resisted the
forming of new cells in the body politic. Except that the drainage
was so temporary as to appear again and again in a series of local
infections in the long-dying of the fundamentalist bent. Perhaps this
is too much again: to call Dayton's trial a spasm, a colic, a carbuncle.
A softer and easier term may well be in better case.

Andrew Dickson White dedicates his great *History of the Warfare
of Science with Theology* to no less a personage than the founder of
Cornell where he wrote the work that covers his subject like a vast
mountain range. But the introduction he wrote in 1895 begins softly
and easily with the *mujiks* picking at the ice in the Neva at St. Peters-
burg to let the sun melt the winter accumulation lest a sudden thaw-
ing of the mass tear out the bridges of the city that span the Neva.

The Scopes trial was a thaw of sorts, but there had been ice pickers
at work for decades. The received theological scheme of things had
been pecked at for more than fifty decades. Even before Copernican
views had been widely received at all the discovery of America had
subjected the theological scheme of things to a terrible strain, says

White,[2] because it made the Ark of Noah such a problem. Whole lifetimes of the work of naturalists were demolished as when the great *Systema Naturae* (1759) of Linnaeus was destroyed in effect by the listing of fifty times as many species of animals as the four thousand he had claimed and the contention that more than half of the species were still unknown—and all this in a hundred years from Linnaeus.

But the real thaw began just 107 years ago on July 1 with two papers in the meeting of the Linnaean Society in London. Here, in the work of Charles Darwin and Alfred Russell Wallace the doctrine of evolution by natural selection came clearly into the modern world from its long gestation in earlier minds. It attracted early support: Sir Charles Lyell's *The Antiquity of Man* (1863), Sir Thomas Huxley's *Man's Place in Nature* (1863). It attracted almost instant support from theologians too. Charles Kingsley wrote to F. D. Maurice as early as 1863, Canon Liddon supported it in his Oxford sermons of 1871. On my desk as I write is the superb series (Bampton Lectures) of the father of William Temple, *The Relations Between Science and Religion,* eight lectures preached before the University of Oxford by the Right Reverend Frederick, Lord Bishop of Exeter, in the year 1884. Here in America, in the stone pulpit where William James later delivered *The Varieties of Religious Experience,* Henry Drummond's *Chautauqua Lectures* (1893) reached a distinguished set of hearers.

But those opposers who focused on Dayton had as formidable a set of antecedent supporters and the theological ice was a barrier. They could and did cite as opposers of Darwin the great Cardinal Manning, Wilberforce, the Bishop of Oxford, the Bishop of Melbourne, Mr. Gladstone, Dr. Pusey, the Society for the Publication of Christian Knowledge, the London *Times,* many American Anglicans, the famous Charles Hodge of Princeton Seminary, and Dr. Noah Porter, president of Yale (with Marsh's great exhibit on the evolution of the horse a stone's throw away, says White), who personally disavowed evolutionary theory as agnostic and pantheistic. But the capstone for Protestant opposition was Pius IX who called these views "repugnant to history, tradition, science, facts, and reason."

2 Andrew Dickson White, *History of the Warfare of Science with Theology* (2 vols.; New York: D. Appleton & Co., 1896), I, 46. Also see the work of the famous Jesuit Joseph Acosta, *Natural and Moral History of the Indies,* 1590.

In spite of all this, evolutionary views penetrated the common thinking of nearly every Southern village. Have you heard the old saw that Darwin's bomb was sixty years exploding in the South? It is not so. By the winter of 1863 on the Rappahannock River in Confederate camps the ordinary Rebel knew a song to the effect that while he, the hardtack and ramrod type, was probably descended from a monkey this certainly did not apply to "Marse Robert" E. Lee!

Meanwhile, and long before Dayton, Darwin died and got himself famously buried by no less a personage than Dean Farrar in Westminster. Almost none of those who wished him dead (or wished at Dayton that he had never lived) had read his two great works or knew that he himself had said: "My brain was never formed for much thinking" or "I look at it as absolutely certain that very much in the *Origin* will be proved rubbish, but I expect and hope that the framework will stand." Or, that years after his father had said, "You care for nothing but shooting, dogs, and rat-catching, and will be a disgrace to yourself and all your family," or that Charles Darwin would say of his life work: "God knows I ought to be thankful for such a perennial interest which makes me forget for some hours every day my accursed stomach."

Not many of Darwin's opposers at Dayton understood that the keystone of the views they fought was cast in terms of a denial of Linnaeus' view (1707–78) that species are immutable; that races or kinds are capable of modification as a result of the successful reproduction of qualities necessary for their survival. Virtually none knew the gracious summary of his own views in his introduction to the *Origin of Species:*

I am fully convinced that species are not immutable; but that those belonging to what are called the same genera are lineal descendants of some other and generally extinct species . . . [and] I am convinced that natural selection has been the main, but not the exclusive means of modification.[3]

What, then, was Dayton's summer? In spite of all excesses of ignorance, piety, and chicanery, the most charitable thing that is neither too much nor too little seems to be that the Dayton trial was "the last significant attempt to discredit Darwin's theory by those

3 Charles Darwin, *Origin of Species* (New York: The Modern Library, 1936), 14.

who sincerely believed that the Biblical story of the creation of man was a complete explanation of the origin of species." [4]

Darrow lost the suit; Mencken paid the fine; but Mr. Bryan died in sleep, and for awhile there was a martyr, second only to Messiah in scores of memorials across the nation. Most eloquent of all, doubtless, was that of the already famous Southern Baptist, Dr. R. G. Lee, who called Bryan,

a mighty statesman eagle, quarreled at but not hindered in his lofty flight, by the noisy human sparrows of his day who envied but could not attain unto his eminence. . . . among the deathless men of all ages. . . . a man in whom the determination of God Almighty burned—our statesman sun by day and our warrior moon by night in every good cause . . . not one gem will ever tarnish in his crown . . . [who] fell in whirlwind, after a stormy conflict with the foes of the Bible.

And then, using the famous "Lincoln lines" that he would use again at the funeral of George W. Truett, Dr. Lee said that Bryan's fall left "a lonesome place against the sky." [5]

III

And what has happened since? Dayton was the end of something —and not much of a beginning to anything—for the forces that help us grow beyond our time and place were already in the environment. Perhaps a few small boys were spurred (almost without remembering Dayton) but that is all. I go through Dayton occasionally on my way back into the Cumberlands of my origins. Some of us have lived there, within ten miles of our original settling, since the year the American Revolution closed and returning Colonials began to take up their land-grants in payment for their decade of service in the Virginia regiment. (Why they left Shenandoah!) There wasn't anything at Dayton then (1789) and there isn't too much now. Bryan University and all the Bryan memorial churches are about as they were—still-born. The evangelist Bob Jones made a beginning at neighboring Cleveland (and the Church of God in one of its branches has a headquarters there), but Jones soon moved his fundamentalist school to Greenville, South Carolina, where his drama and music departments at least show a good hand at programming radio funda-

---

4 George I. Schwartz and Philip W. Bishop (eds.), *Moments of Discovery* (2 vols.; New York: Basic Books, 1958), II, 659.
5 R. G. Lee, *A Chosen Vessel* (Grand Rapids, Mich.: Zondervan, 1949), 155.

mentalism. But there he is under the shadow of old Furman from whence for a hundred years a good solid stream of enlightened freedmen has been emerging. There was an Episcopalian lay-woman in sociology there for forty years who produced a stream of emancipated students like Kyle Haselden (an eighth generation South Carolinian), and men like all the Poteats, the Edward McDowells, the Fred Noes, the Dean E. A. Tibbses, and the Charles Burtses, who have graced its faculty and student rosters. Multiply Furman by a hundred, include the state schools, the land grant colleges, the Mercers and Maryvilles and Bereas which have fed the graduate schools from Chicago to Harvard, poll their present faculties, and Dayton recedes to the terminal point of a dying fundamentalist bent that did not really die but never mattered much.

But for one brief moment during a long hot summer, Dayton seemed to hold promise of being the locale for a *Götterdämmerung* of Appalachia's gods. But not really. The same gods are still there. Meanwhile, the better and bigger story would be of the replacement of private power with TVA. This had more to do with any change in theology the region enjoys than Dayton had. For time of itself changes nothing—only new experience can change us—the rearing of dams and power plants, the introduction of new techniques and minds, the raising up of chemical and textile and synthetic fabric mills has made the Tennessee Valley hum, if not to rejoice. And Oak Ridge, sprawling across fields my mother knew as blackberry patches, is the center of an incredible concentration, where last January I sat with six hundred specialists in nuclear studies from the entire free-world to watch and hear a native-son from the Sahara of Bozart talk a lingo I could neither translate nor remember.

I know Lone Oak, in Paducah, too, at the mouth of the same Tennessee River. I learned all I know about poverty and hope and native dignity in a huge old people's church where I once tried to serve as pastor. And Lone Oak, where the boy John Scopes went to school, has not changed much, but the enemy was and is not poor Darwin. For where have the established churches had a harder time of it than Appalachia? Not because the native man is a *sectarian*. He is natively *agnostic*. His free-thinkers in the mills and shops question everything, especially strangers, still. And the real mountaineer is devout only when overcome by example, and experience. (An air force sergeant in Wilmington taught me the first public prayer of his old bootlegger uncle who attended a prayer service at Cades Cove:

> O God, if there is any,
> Forgive my sins, if I've done any,
> And when I die, if I ever do,
> Take me to be with you—
>   if you want to. Amen.)

The effect of Dayton on the fundamentalist bent? I say "bent" because fundamentalism is not a rational position or a logical theology, though it has its premise, its rationale, and its literal equational format. Fundamentalism is emotive, a bias, a provincialism that new information cannot change. It is a *neurosis*. But if it is, the old so-called liberalism is its opposite and an emotive problem too, a *psychosis*. It's as bad to have one's window stuck open as it is to have it stuck shut. In either event of extreme one loses the use of the window. Some things simply never mattered less and both are illnesses from which we need a healing, a being made whole. The release from any regionalism, either in theology or science, requires an understanding of symbols. And practically no one had this in the Tennessee of the twenties. Neither Bryan, nor Darrow, nor any of the fundamentalists, nor their "liberal" tormentors understood the nature of language. Both were literalists of the same type. The only thing more disgraceful than Mr. Bryan's answers at Dayton was the set of Mr. Darrow's questions. The quality of both question and answer reveals an ignorance of language, myth, and meaning as appalling as the whole set-up was sordidly unreal and shameful. Nothing could have been won there. Nothing was at stake. The questions had changed already. And the most hopeless thing on earth was the thought that the brilliant statements of the able, devout, Professor Kirtley F. Mather, the gracious agnostic W. C. Curtis, and the other specialists like Fay-Cooper Cole could have been heard in such a caterwauling din as the Baal-grove the Dayton courthouse lawn had become when "court" was moved outside.

Nothing, then, was settled at Dayton. Professor Mather says that the old Tennessee law may still hang over the heads of timid young teachers like the "Sword of Damocles." I doubt it. The useless law is not so heavy. It never was this heavy. It is no more a weight than the still existent Massachusetts law against whipping one's wife with a stick thicker than one's thumb. Laws do not get their weight as law by being on the books. Laws are only laws as they reflect and feed back the real mores and values of a people. I doubt if anyone ever took the Tennessee law against teaching evolutionary theory very seriously, especially the legislators who enacted it. They knew it was for consumption "back home" just as clearly as some of those Texas legislators I used to fight in the halls at Austin knew their thirteen bad racist bills on the floor were for the county papers in East Texas, not for permanent *Law*. Both are disgraceful, just like the present oath-law in North Carolina state colleges, written by a secretary of state who does not know one denies freedom by coercing its "protection." The law itself made no difference to a people who from Anglo-Saxon sources cared for only one law: the law against trespass. It reads, "Thou shalt not trespass on a neighbor's land, his cattle, or his woman," and this covers everything. Notice this particularly in the rate of enforcement of the school attendance law, the fantastically amusing effort to control the production of "white" whiskey, and watch its demonstration in the areas where the only civil rights available have been taken up by the rare freedman who has achieved an acknowledged manhood. The old Tennessee law was never law and never mattered. It was a flag, but that is all. Dayton settled nothing. The forces of change were other than courts can deal with and were already, slowly, in ferment.

Of course there was a wildness in the twenties which the Dayton episode reflects. In the South, except for islands where their students served, there was almost total rejection of Walter Rauschenbusch and the social gospel, of Shailer Mathews and the Chicago liberals. Biblical criticism was *German* and modern. (Though John R. Sampey gave me Old Testament views much more advanced than those for which Ralph Elliot was fired at Kansas City two years ago.) There was also, even among Presbyterians, a rejection and restriction of social customs and functions. (When Davidson trustees tried to prevail upon the brilliant and caustic Kenneth Foreman to join the faculty in throwing a "restraining influence" upon the student dances then held in Charlotte hotels, he remarked that he found it a trifle difficult to throw a "restraint" seventeen miles!) But this sweep of conservatism in the twenties was a recurrence that featured the re-appearances of other forces from the 1870's–90's. On the back of a reconstruction that did not reconstruct and a hatred region-wide of the immovable Grover Cleveland (see Mencken's fine characterization), there was the Ku Klux Klan in all its sordid equippage. The Klan came back in the twenties, the fifties, and sixties (though a crowd of Pembroke Indians with shotguns "dispersed" its rally near their Carolina headquarters recently). Along with these, the tenets of mid-Western and Southern WASP-iness (White, Anglo-Saxon, Protestant), the anti-everything baiters, the off-beat publishers, and the tons of hate literature which name everyone from Oxnam to Eisenhower as Communist, the Texas brand of neo-fascism, the McCarthy-type use of our paranoid fears, all, as in the present time, seems to have run together for a great *Festschrift* at Dayton in the twenties, but it was no worse than now, I think, and no better. Although the Presbyterians fired their brilliant President James Woodrow from the Columbia seminary and ruled that no man under rule of presbytery could study under him at the University of South Carolina, the Baptists never quite got to E. Y. Mullins, who spoke of "progressive" revelation to keep from saying "evolutionary." Then, too, he moved successfully the famous "previous question" at Memphis, and the new statement of faith, which did not say what it said, was passed and the crisis dimmed. Dayton was lost in the late twenties rustle of professors moving out and up from denominational schools to state schools and in the closing-off of provincial pastor's minds by the desire to have no trouble, like the candidate for a school in Morgan County who, when asked whether he believed the earth was round or four-cornered, said, "Brethren, I am fully prepared to teach her either way!" All this is to say that Dayton was an episode, in a time as wild as the present, which sparked at best a few young inquirers in their move to a clearer light and which revealed then and reflects now the caustic, hurtful fact that the sources of light and change and redemption did not then and do not now reside in the great denominational houses that advertise to have them for distribution. The real salvation of the Tennessee Valley will come neither from a Dayton courtroom nor the Protestant denominational ghettos. And the region has still the task of reaching very far beyond its time and place. John Scopes was then, and is still, the keenest mind to judge at Dayton. He saw the summer for what it was and walked away into a useful and a helpful anonymity.

IV

And what is the hope for a region to grow beyond its time and place? What is happening in the South?

In his current study of the life of the respected theologian W. T. Conner, a native of the Southwest, Professor Stewart A. Newman says that "it is next to impossible to know any institution apart from the (cultural) circumstances of its birth." The backdrop of every story is the way persons, institutions, religions are affected by the milieu their region affords. We are products of our time and place. "No man *ever* lives ahead of his time," said the grizzled and beautiful Negro veteran, Benjamin Mays, with stunning effect in my Charlotte pulpit. Of the churches it is true that none could exist in a vacuum. All churches pick up and are picked up by and reflect the provincialism that spawned them. This is both our secret and our shame—a kind of shameful secret. If you know our localisms you know us—and anywhere persons transcend their localisms to join a larger world they do so in an agony of separation and tension. Arnold Toynbee said (May 10, 1964) in the New York *Times,* that his lifetime agony had been the attempt to grow beyond his own time and place. "The navel of my earth is not in Greece," he says, but it is around the comically ugly and reassuringly familiar Albert Memorial in Kensington Gardens. "One is a prisoner of one's time and place," and "what a bore one's own native civilization is"—and yet, his real and more formidable reason for disliking the West is that in Toynbee's own lifetime the West has produced: two world wars, communism, National Socialism, fascism, Mussolini, McCarthy, Hitler (and if Britain's cousins can murder six million Jews what cannot Britain do?). Add our culture-wide crimes—individualism, callousness toward the aged—our standardizations, our love of speed, mass production, our premature sexuality, and our splintering of genuine universals—and where can a man go? I find this provincial bit even and especially in Cambridge, but I have a deeper quarrel than Toynbee's. The West has tried to teach us all that we can provide our own security. It has taught us to blink at life's facts! And Dayton helped.

And our hope? It begins in the prospect of understanding our own self-images, claims my associate, Robert E. McClernon. Kenneth Scott Latourette, one of the grandest friends the Southern church has had, said on the boardwalk at Atlantic City that every time he comes South he has to change his stereotype! One escapes the limitations of his Daytons only as he comes to understand his own self-stereotypes.

At this writing I have just come from a historic "Jubilee" meeting of two major religious bodies (seven conventions) separated for over a hundred years. We met simultaneously and alongside, under the same roof. The exhibits covered acres and the chairs were twenty thousand. Both crowds were produced by identical causes:

the responses of a people to their own time and place. And we saw, by incredibly narrow margins, in the Southern group the nervous triumph of a *regionalism,* a volk-neurosis, which, when threatened in its time and place, rejected any prospect of change from outside (just as did the Southern Presbyterians) and refused to face specific issues like racism with such inane substitutes that Warren Carr of Durham protested he would rather see us say nothing at all than this potage of shibboleths about the Holy Ghost and local autonomy!

Forty years beyond Dayton what keeps us like this? We are products of our time and place. The old Confederate gods rose from their graves. The pastors of the same pulpits which a hundred years ago were exhorting the South to follow war-gods two years past the point of exhaustion—cried out again, "You will damage us." So, by less than 100 plurality, we voted to damage instead the lesser churches who must make their flight almost alone on social issues.

Mark us off? Mark it all off. Not much would be lost if the "Sahara of Bozart" disappeared. But provincialism will not go with our going anymore than with Dayton's passing forty years ago. I said once that the Southern churches (of all denominations) are mainly Jesus-cults dressed in the Little Lord Fauntleroy clothing of our Confederate narcissism, and have been editorially berated from Los Angeles to Denver to Jackson in the religious press. But no one remembered that the next sentence claimed that the churches north of God were choking too on that other unitarianism—that of a sterile Father who has no children left at all! We are all victims and veterans of our time and place. Mark us off!

But if our ghettos are ever abandoned change will come as fast as summer lightning across a dark sky. Some of us wait around the region because in any reversal of a retreat those in the van become advance pickets for a new assault. So we watch and pray some—since Dayton and Atlantic City—that, as a famous Northerner said to me, our sister churches may not be swallowed by their urban sociological nemesis or consumed by a smugness of the heart.

And what is our hope of change now? It rests in pilot churches, schools, and teachers, who can understand the times and places that have made our stereotyped self-images. This exciting, unnerving, volatile place in which six of us are set down as clergy-colleagues is a case in point for a New South. Who are we? We are not yet legion, but there is one of us in every Southern city. Here we are twenty-eight denominations, eight nationalities, four ethnic groups, four principal regions, and two races. We are *every* class, but principally we are a *new* class. We, here, in the New South, are a macrocosmos of everything in the New World. We are only about ten years from Dayton and frontier pietism. We are barely out of Babbitry and Elmer Gantryism. We have high technological education, medium cultural aspirations, and are now, in North Carolina, a respectable address. We are novices in the higher expressions of the Christian religion. We haven't even, as yet, a common Book, and are barely emerging into a concept of our world-church responsibilities. Two thirds of us grew up with a "Southern" mind. That is to say, in the tradition of Burke and Adams, Randolph and Calhoun, we were and are still partly believers in slow processes of natural change; we have deep regard for agricultural traditions; we are assertively individualistic; we have an uneasy awareness of two races; we think local government means less change; we would like a real aristocracy of classes and orders; and we would love to be able to believe in a Divine Order for Society that would sanction our prejudices, proscriptions, and presumptions. Our tendencies press us into a romantic nostalgia that wishes to keep some of the magnolia blossoms from that world that never was. We are attracted to that noveau-culturalism in which men are reaching for values of which they are not yet sure. Our psuedo-cosmopolitanism serves to cover the guilt in which we try our freedom in daring new social practices heretofore *verboten*. Our philistinism makes us still fiercely protective of purely local values. Fundamentally, our religious needs (we think) are for inspiration to help us retread old moral decisions and for reconfirmation of our old religious hopes. We dread, we shrink from the new responsibility of the laity and we still expect our hired holy men to "lead out" by telling us things to do, furnishing answers, and blessing the culture that sustains us. Most everywhere the good professionals can do this without preaching over our heads.

It is with this kind of luggage in our wagon that we have set out upon our journey toward a relevant expression of real Christian faith and where we continue to exist at all we are a miracle!

By all the laws of a recognizable sociology we should have swamped in Confederate seas, or been stove-in by the reefs of the religious conservatism we keep passing, or blown up from our own inner stresses. That we are not becalmed, aground, or broken yet is a miracle due to a climate we did not create recently. It was around our fathers, too, this urge to go beyond our time and place. This is no recent change of weather. And our survival is due to a *corps,* a fellowship sparked by priest and lay who know more, love more, are permissive with each other and are, here and there, possessors of that charisma without which no spirit can survive in hostile seas.

Do we represent a New South? We do not have to ask, or care. We represent the new human race that is dropping its concern with adjectives like Baptist or White or Southern. And those who do not give us up or are not forced into the new Huguenot Expulsion going on in every major denomination, those who are truly pilgrims with us, while entertaining no hope that Baptists per se can be saved from their emotional authoritarianism and pseudo-pragmaticism, or Presbyterians from their pre-World War I orthodoxy, or Methodists from their cultural prison, or Episcopalians from Nirvana, still welcome from all these households of decadent faith refugees such as have come across that bit of insight David put in his "last" song when old and full of years, he said, in effect,

> He that leadeth a people
>   must transcend his own place and time
>   with simplicity and a universal belongingness
>   that permeates like sunshine after early
>   rain, like morning dew.

Says David (God's darling), at the end, my house isn't like this yet, but we have a covenant.

For us, as for John Scopes, Dayton can go now. We have other journeys we must take.

APPENDIXES

Affidavit Read to the Court at Dayton, Tennessee, July 20, 1925

WINTERTON C. CURTIS

Nature and Current Aspects of the Doctrine of Evolution

Definitions are wearisome. But we may ask ourselves, by way of limitation, what is evolution in general and organic evolution in particular. The answer can best be given by means of illustrations. The term evolution, as today used in science, means the historical process of change. When we speak of the evolution of man-made products, like automobiles and steam engines, of social institutions like democratic government, of the crust of our earth, of solar systems, of animals and plants, we mean a gradual coming into existence of what is now before us, in contrast to its sudden and miraculous creation. Such an idea is of recent origin. Our intellectual forbears of a few centuries ago thought in terms of a world created in its present form. The evolutionary point of view marked an advance from the concept of a static universe to one that is dynamic. In the phraseology of the street, the world is a going concern, historically as well as in its present aspects.

Evolution is, therefore, the doctrine of how things have changed in the past and how they are changing in the present. It may be naturally divided into its cosmic, geologic, and organic aspects, as represented by the sciences of astronomy, geology and biology.

Cosmic Evolution

Cosmic evolution includes all other forms, for by the cosmic we mean the entire visible universe, our very bodies, as well as the farthest star. But in practice, one thinks of the cosmos as remote. And what we have in mind under cosmic evolution are the changes that are postulated by the science of astronomy. It is believed by astronomers that our solar system with its central sun, its planets and lesser bodies, has not always possessed its present form, although it has been in existence from a remote period of time. Our earth seems to have been once molten, and before that perhaps gaseous. Although the famous nebular hypothesis of Laplace has been in part replaced by other theories, the belief of modern astronomers is that our solar system and perhaps countless others have arisen by an evolutionary process whose extent is infinite in both time and space. I take it that few will combat the concepts of astronomy regarding the nature of our sun and planets. Even when some of us were children the idea of cosmic evolution, as set forth by the nebular hypothesis, the plantesimal hypothesis, or the like is correct, but that the astronomer regards the heavenly bodies as having reached their present state by an evolutionary stage continuous through an unfathomable past and presumably to be continued into a limitless future. There is no longer talk among intelligent or educated men—or there should not be—of "heaven, earth, center and circumference, created all together, in the same instant, and clouds full of water, on October 23, in the year 4004 B.C. at 9 o'clock in the morning" as was determined by the chronology of Dr. John Lightfoot in the seventeenth century. The astronomical evidence for the development of such a dynamic universe in space and time is of course limited. But it all points in the direction of evolution.

Geologic Evolution

Geologic evolution overlaps with cosmic, since the geologist takes the evolutionary problem where the astronomer leaves it. Geology deals with the history of our earth, how it originated and how it has assumed its present form. Astronomy deals with the origin of the earth as a planet of our solar system. Geology finds evidence that the earth was once a molten mass which has since been "cooled." What may be called the "countenance" of the earth is the subject matter of geology, how the land lies at the present day, how rocks and soil are being produced, and what these facts imply regarding historical origins. The evolutionary evidence of astronomy is vague and remote, although generally accepted by the layman. The evidence from geology is written in the ground beneath our feet. The geologist's belief in a vast lapse of time and stupendous changes rests upon evidence that is everywhere at hand. Leonardo da Vinci, in the fifteenth century, grasped the significance of important geological facts, when he wrote concerning the saltiness of the sea and the marine shells found as fossils in the high mountains. Since the publication of James Hutton's *Theory of the Earth,* in 1795, it has been the cardinal principle of geological science that past changes of the earth's surface are explicable in terms of changes now in operation. For example, such a vast chasm as the Grand Canyon is explained not as produced by miraculous creation or by sudden catastrophe, but by running water acting upon the rocks throughout innumerable centuries. The process may be observed in miniature in the wash of the soil in Tennessee fields. The weathering of rock into soil, erosion with its transportation of the products of weathering, deposition of the material in the oceans or in large bodies of fresh water, uplift of the ocean's floor and its hardening into rock may all be seen in slow but certain progress in various parts of the world at the present day, and their occurrence in the past is recorded in the rocks. The subtitle of Charles Lyell's famous book, the *Principles of Geology*, published in 1830, runs as follows: "An attempt to explain the former changes of the earth's surface by reference to causes now in operation." Lyell established the idea of evolution as the only reasonable interpretation of geological facts and his elaboration of Hutton's doctrines still constitute the very foundation of geologic science. Today, geology without an evolution of the earth's surface from a molten mass to its present form, and extending over millions of years, would be on a par with a science of geography postulating a flat earth. The conclusions of modern astronomy and geology, therefore, point to an evolutionary process—involving many millions of years and still in progress—to an earth hoary with age and still growing old.

Astronomy and geology, despite their practical importance, are remote from human concern, insofar as their evolutionary doctrines are concerned. To borrow from the phraseology of a distinguished anti-evolutionist, the age of the rocks is of no particular consequence insofar as the Rock of Ages is concerned. Cosmic evolution and geologic evolution are readily accepted by the laity on the authority of science, because they do not seriously interfere with doctrines that are deemed vital. But the evolution of plant and animal life, and hence human evolution, is inseparable from that of inorganic matter as described by astronomy and geology, because of the fossils in the rocks.

Organic Evolution

Organic evolution resembles the cosmic and geologic evolution described above since it concludes that the living bodies, which are the objects of its investigation, have not always existed as they are today, but have undergone a process of change. As with the evidence of geologic change, the evidence for an evolution of animals and plants rests upon facts that are immediately before us, for example, the structure and development of animals, their distribution over the earth, the fossils in the rocks. Our time will permit only enumeration and brief characterization of the recognized lines of evidence for organic evolution, which are as follows:

First—Evidence from structure is derived from:
    Comparative anatomy.
    Comparative embryology.
    Classification.
Second—Evidence from distribution, past and present, is derived from:
    Paleontology.
    Zoogeography.
Third—Evidence from physiology is derived from:
    Fundamental resemblances in vital processes.
    Specific chemical resemblances of closely related forms; e.g., blood
        tests.

Fourth—Evidence from experimentation rests upon:
    Unconscious experimentation upon animals and plants since their domestication.
    Conscious experimentation of breeders and of scientific investigators.

The nature of these lines of evidence may now be indicated.

Evidence from Comparative Anatomy—In the animal kingdom as a whole and in every group of animals, whether large or small, we find facts that may be interpreted most reasonably in terms of evolution. The vertebrates or backboned animals will serve as an illustration. We find here a certain plan of structure, for example, backbone, two pairs of limbs, body, head and various internal organs, all laid down according to a similar general plan, but with endless modifications to suit the mode of life. The flipper of a whale, the wing of a bird or a bat, the forefoot of a horse, the arm of a man, and the like, all show the same plan of structure. One of the pre-Darwin ideas was that each animal, while created separately, was nevertheless formed in accordance with a certain type that the Creator had in mind, hence the resemblance. Such an idea is a theoretical possibility, provided there is any evidence to show that animals were created all at once and separately. But there is not a shred of such evidence that will appeal to one who approaches the matter with an open mind and uninfluenced by preconceived notions.

On the other hand, the biological explanation of this anatomical resemblance is that the present vertebrates (fishes, amphibia, reptiles, birds and mammals) have all descended from a primitive race, somewhat like the present fishes. All vertebrates are now alike, because they have never lost the underlying plan of structure inherited from their common ancestry. They have come honestly and naturally by present organization.

The Evidence from Fossils (Paleontology)—Interlocks with the above, since the first vertebrates known to appear were primitive fishlike forms. These were succeeded by amphibians, reptiles, mammals and birds in the order named, the last two having connecting links with the reptiles. The invertebrate groups tell a similar story.

The Facts of Comparative Embryology—The kind of evidence everywhere discoverable may be illustrated by the gill-slits in the embryos of higher vertebrates like reptiles, birds and mammals. All these forms exhibit in their early stages of development a fishlike plan of structure, particularly in the neck region where the gill-slits are located. The reasonable interpretation of the existence of such structures in the embryo of a human being, or any land-living vertebrate, is that we have never lost this tell-tale evidence of our ancestry. The later stages of our development are modified so that they lead to the adult human body. The earlier stages still show the primitive conditions of a fishlike organization. Modern fishes have survived to the present day without a fundamental departure from the ancestral condition. Modern amphibia (frogs, toads and salamanders) have survived in the halfway state between an aquatic and a terrestrial existence, through which higher vertebrates have passed as indicated by the fossil record and by the above fishlike stages in their development.

The facts of classification are commonly cited as evidence for evolution. Since classification is based on structure (anatomy), this is but an aspect of the general evidence from comparative anatomy and embryology. While the facts cannot be detailed here, they are striking and bear out the doctrine.

Another line of evidence is that of geological geographical distribution. The facts in this connection are utterly senseless and insulting to an intelligent creator, if viewed as a result of special creation. One can simply say, "God did it," and not ask why. But such explanations do not satisfy modern minds. On the other hand, their explanation in terms of evolution give reasonableness and consistency to a large body of facts. The fossils appear in such an order in time as to constitute evidence for evolution. Existing animals are distributed over the surface of the earth in a manner that confirms their geological origins.

The facts of physiology tell a similar story. Life and the living stuff is the same sort of thing wherever we find it, thus lending support to the idea that it has all descended from the same primitive source from which it has inherited its resemblances. A more striking line of physiological evidence is the recently discovered chemical resemblance between the blood of animals previously supposed to be closely related on grounds of their anatomical similarities, for example, apes and monkeys, birds and reptiles and the like. Two entirely independent lines of evidence are here found to interlock to such an extent that evolution is the one reasonable interpretation.

Evidence from Experimentation

Finally there is the evidence from experimentation: Evolution has taken place before the eyes of men, during the period since animals and plants were first domesticated. The changes have not been profound, because the ten or twenty thousand years since the first animals and plants seem to have been brought under domestication is a brief span of time for evolutionary modification. But it is clear that such modification has occurred and is today occurring under the direction of skillful breeders. The modern science of genetics is beginning to solve the problem of how evolution takes place, although this question is one of extreme difficulty.

The foregoing summary of the various lines of evidence is hopelessly inadequate, since books could be written on each. The point to be appreciated is that all the multitudinous facts of biology hang together in a consistent fashion when viewed in terms of evolution, while they are meaningless when considered as the arbitrary acts of a creator who brought them into existence all at once a few thousand years in the past. Modern biology has developed around two major generalizations, the cell doctrine, and the doctrine of organic evolution. Modern evolutionism dates not from Darwin's *Origin of Species,* published in 1859, but from the historic *Naturello* of Buffon, the first volume of which appeared in 1749, and from the work of the other philosopher-naturalists of the eighteenth century. It is a sad comment upon the state of popular information that the practical facts of biological science are everywhere acknowledged, while the status of its greatest philosophical generalization remains so commonly unknown. In view of its implications and applications, the doctrine of evolution is second to none in modern thought, it has been established by a gradual but irresistible accumulation of facts.

At this point, we may examine a common misunderstanding with reference to evolution and the work of Charles Darwin. Suppose we begin with an analogy, illustrating what may be termed the fact, the course and the causes in a progressive series of events. A ship leaves a European port for the New York harbor. We may distinguish between: (1) The fact that the ship actually crossed the ocean, instead of being "created" in the harbor of New York; (2) the course the ship may have pursued, whether direct or indirect, and the like; and (3) the causes that made the ship go, whether an internal propelling force like steam or electricity, an external force like wind or current or even direction by wireless. Compared with the doctrine of evolution, we have: (1) the fact of evolution, as representing the historical series of events; (2) the course followed in evolution, for instance, whether the land vertebrates arose from the fishlike ancestors, birds from reptiles, or the like; and (3) the causes of evolution or what made and makes it happen. These three aspects, like those in the voyage of a ship, are separate though related items. They must be constantly distinguished if there is to be any clear thinking on this matter by one who is not a scientist.

It is now possible to explain the misunderstanding above cited. The historical fact of evolution seems attested by overwhelming evidence. Science has nothing to conceal, it stands "strong in the strength of demonstrable facts," and invites you to view the evidence. The course pursued by evolution is known broadly in many instances, but in the nature of the case the evidence is limited and many of the steps will always remain uncertain, without, however, a calling in question of the historic fact. The causes of evolution present the most difficult problem of all and the one regarding which we know the least. The recent strictures of Professor Bateson, which have been exploited by anti-evolutionists, were directed wholly at current explanations of evolutionary causation and the course of evolution. He affirmed his belief in the historic fact when he said "our faith in evolution is unshaken"—meaning by "faith," of course, a reasonable belief resting upon evidence.

That such an interpretation of Professor Bateson's views is the correct one appears from the following communication:

11 December, 1922,
The Manor House,
Merton,
London, S. W. 20.

DEAR PROFESSOR CURTIS:

The papers you have sent me relating to the case of Mr. —— give a curious picture of life under democracy. We may count ourselves happy if we are not all hanged like the Clerk of Chatham, with our pens and ink horns about our necks!

I have looked through my Toronto address again. I see nothing in it which can be construed as expressing doubt as to the main fact of evolution. In the last paragraph (copy enclosed) you will find a statement in the most explicit words I could find giving the opinion which appears to me forced upon us by the facts—an opinion shared, I supposed, by every man of science in the world.

At Toronto I was addressing an audience, mainly professional. I took occasion to call the attention of my colleagues to the loose thinking and unproven assumptions which pass current as to the actual processes of evolution. We do know that the plants and animals, including most certainly man, have been evolved from other and very different forms of life. As to the nature of this process of evolution, we have many conjectures, but little positive knowledge. That is as much of the matter as can be made clear without special study, as you and I very well know.

The campaign against the teaching of evolution is a terrible example of the way in which truth can be perverted by the ignorant. You may use as much of this letter as you like and I hope it may be of service.

Very truly,

W. BATESON

The paragraph to which Professor Bateson refers above is the concluding one of his address and runs as follows:

I have put before you very frankly the considerations which have made us agnostic as to the actual mode and processes of evolution. When such confessions are made the enemies of science see their chance. If we cannot declare here and now how species arose, they will obligingly offer us the solutions with which obscurantism is satisfied. Let us then proclaim in precise and unmistakable language that our faith in evolution is unshaken. Every available line of argument converges on this inevitable conclusion. The obscurantist has nothing to suggest which is worth a moment's attention. The difficulties which weigh upon the professional biologist need not trouble the layman. Our doubts are not as to the reality or truth of evolution, but as to the origin of species, a technical, almost domestic, problem. Any day that mystery may be solved. The discoveries of the last twenty-five years enable us for the first time to discuss these questions intelligently and on a basis of fact. That synthesis will follow on an analysis we do not and cannot doubt.

With this distinction between fact, course and causes clearly in mind, the significance of Darwin's work in the history of biological thought can be understood. Darwin's accomplishment was two-fold. In the first place he established organic evolution as the only reasonable explanation of the past history of living things. Secondly, he offered, in natural selection, what then appeared an adequate explanation for the origin of species, and hence for the causes of evolution. Darwin's evolutionary argument in his *Origin of Species* was that one species could give rise to another "by means" as he believed, "of natural selection or the preservation of favored races in the struggle for life." If one species could be shown to give rise to another, the same process could be continued. No limit could be set. The types thus produced could depart indefinitely from the parent form. Once the mutability of species be admitted the only reasonable conclusion is that evolution has taken place. His argument was supported by an immense collection of facts along observational and experimental lines. The total result was overwhelming, coming as it did more than 100 years after the setting forth of transmutation, and its repeated rejection by the main body of naturalists. Evolution was accepted so quickly by scientists that the world was startled. This sudden conversion gave rise to the impression, even among scientific workers, that no serious contribution to evolutionary theory had been made before the work of Darwin. Such an impression does not represent the facts and it does grave injustice to the pioneer thinkers of the eighteenth century, to whom we have alluded.

Darwin's second accomplishment, natural selection, was accepted by science as a causo-mechanical explanation of evolutionary change. The cogent statement and the simplicity of the principle of selection were of great importance for its acceptance as the cause of evolution, along with the broader theory of evolution as the historic fact. Extended exposition of the selection process will not be attempted. It may be found in numerous elementary books, and in the early chapters of the *Origin of Species*. The tabulation known as Wallace's chart, which is an admirable outline of the argument, may be cited in this connection:

Wallace's Chart of Natural Selection

Proved Facts—(a) Rapid increase of numbers;
             (b) total numbers stationary;
             (c) struggle for existence;
             (d) variation and heredity;
             (e) survival of the fittest;
             (f) change of environment.
Consequences—Struggle for existence;
             survival of the fittest (natural selection);
             structural modifications.

The importance of Darwin's work in the history of scientific thought is that it convinced science of the truth of organic evolution and proposed a then plausible theory of evolutionary causation. Since Darwin's time, evolution as the historic fact has received confirmation on every hand. It is now regarded by competent scientists as the only rational explanation of an overwhelming mass of facts. Its strength lies in the extent to which it gives meaning to so many phenomena that would be meaningless without such a hypothesis.

But the case of natural selection is far different. Of recent years this theory of the causes of evolution has suffered a decline. No other hypothesis, however, has completely displaced it. It remains the most satisfactory explanation of the origin of adaptations, although its all-sufficiency is no longer accepted. The initial step in evolution is the appearance of individual variations which are perpetuated by heredity rather than by the selection of variations after they have appeared. The interest of investigators has shifted to problems of variation and heredity, as exemplified by the rise of the science of genetics.

As a result of this situation, there has been much discussion among scientists regarding the adequacy of what is often referred to as the Darwinian theory, meaning natural selection. In condemning selection as an inadequate explanation of the problem, biologists have often seemed to condemn evolution itself. It is not strange that the layman, for whom Darwinism and evolution are synonymous terms, believes that evolution has been rejected when he hears that belief in Darwinism is on the wane. He does not understand that what is thus meant by Darwinism is not the historic fact of evolution, but the proposed cause of evolution—natural selection. This point may not seem vital, but those interested in biological science frequently find the situation used to support claims that the entire concept of organic evolution has fallen into disrepute. There are many, even today, who rejoice at anything that appears to weaken this major generalization of biology.

Such then is the more strictly scientific status of the doctrine of evolution as a whole. The origin, by evolution, of the heavenly bodies and of our earth is evidenced by facts of astronomy and geology, as set forth in any elementary treatise on these sciences. Inorganic evolution, or the modification of nonliving matter, is thus supported by science and does not find serious opposition in the public mind. Organic evolution, or the origin of animal and plant life, receives a similar support from the facts of biology. If the origin of man were not involved, there would be presumably little serious opposition from nonscientific sources of the present day.

Human Evolution

But with the evolution of all other living things, both animal and plant, overwhelmingly attested by the facts, it is not only impossible, but puerile to separate man from the general course of events. Moreover, the evidence for man's origin is becoming clearer year by year. Comparative anatomy, embryology, classification, physiology, geographical distribution, fossils and the existing races of mankind tell the same story for man as for the rest of the animal world.

Huxley's essay, entitled *Man's Place in Nature,* presents in a masterful manner the anatomical evidence for our kinship with the four species of tailless apes—the gibbon, gorilla, orang and chimpanzee—and his most significant conclusions are even more strongly established at the present day. If creation occurred at 9:00 A.M. on October 23rd of the year 4004 B.C., as part of the divine plan, it is amazing that such success should have dogged the steps of the students of human skeletal and cultural remains during the last half-century. The skeletons, in part or in whole, are known for a number of subhuman races and a vast array of implements and other remains, all showing a progressive advancement. By another fifty years it seems safe to expect that much more of the story will be unveiled. It is further amazing that investigations in Egypt show the existence of a flourishing civilization in the Nile Valley as early as 5000 B.C., and back of this a gradual development from the barbarism of the Stone Age.

On man's intellectual side, psychology is making increasingly evident the essential animal foundation of human intelligence. Man's claim to importance in the universe, revealed by science, lies not in the pretense that this planet was created for his convenience, but in the claim that he transcends the material universe in so far as he comprehends it. And the method of such comprehension that dominates modern thought is the method of science, not that of theology.

The question of human beginnings is one that is open to investigation, like any other historic or prehistoric event. In this connection a quotation from a famous essay by Herbert Spencer, published in 1852, is appropriate: "Those who cavalierly reject the theory of evolution," writes Spencer, "as not adequately supported by facts seem quite to forget that their own theory is supported by no facts at all. Like the majority of men who are born to a given belief, they demand the most rigorous proof of any adverse belief, but assume that their own needs none. Here we find, scattered over the globe, vegetable and animal organisms numbering of the one kind (according to Humboldt), some 320,000 species, and of the other some 2,000,000 species (see Carpenter); and if to these we add the numbers of animals and vegetable species that have become extinct, we may safely estimate the number of species that have existed, and are existing on the earth, at not less than 10,000,000. Well, which is the most rational theory about these 10,000,000 species? Is it most likely that there have been 10,000,000 special creations? Or is it most likely that by continual modifications, due to a change of circumstances, 10,000,000 of varieties have been produced, as varieties are being produced still?

And, one might add, if the evidence indicates that all other species have arisen by evolution, it is probable that man, whose bodily structure and functions are so nearly identical with those of the mammalia and particularly the primates—that man arose in a different fashion. We have, moreover, as above indicated, the positive evidence to support this general presumption.

And having outlined the evidence for human evolution and stated the presumption in its favor, let us turn to the evidence for special creation, as found in Genesis. Science and common sense alike inquire regarding the nature and sources of this account, if it be regarded as a true statement of the facts. Science faces the matter squarely, desiring only the right to investigate and draw unprejudiced conclusions. The results of such investigations are not in doubt. It appears that the races about the eastern Mediterranean, like other primitive peoples, had their traditions of the origin of the world. The story in Genesis apparently descended to the early Hebrews and to their neighbors in Mesopotamia from a source far antedating the appearance of the Jews as a people and their sacred writings. Archeology and ethnology most reasonably indicate that in its origin this

Hebrew-Babylonian tradition may be compared with the stories of many primitive peoples. We take the story in Genesis seriously as an account of prehistorical facts, because it is our story of creation passed down by tradition from our fathers. It is, and will remain, sacred and interesting, because it has been woven into the thought of Western culture for almost 2,000 years and because of its intrinsic literary and moral qualities.

But the past history of events, whether of human or animal origins, is subject matter for scientific inquiry, and the answer of science is evolution. The very great antiquity of man, the existence at an earlier period of beings, manlike, but intermediate between man and other primates, together with the facts of man's anatomy, his embryology, his physiological reactions, even his mentality, all point to his bodily kinship with the rest of living nature. It is not that men came from monkeys, but that men, monkeys and apes all came from a common mammalian ancestry millions of years in the past.

It is more reasonable to believe that the Bible is a human document representing the history of an advance from the concept of a barbarous and vengeful Jehovah of the earlier Old Testament, through the God of righteousness and justice of the later prophets, and culminating in the concept of a Father as preached by Jesus of Nazareth.

In the foregoing statement we have considered the intellectual aspects of the doctrine of organic evolution. There remains its social aspects. Evolution is one of the basic concepts in modern thought. Suppression of a doctrine established by such overwhelming evidence is a serious matter. From the standpoint of the teacher the situation has more than academic interest.

Evolution has been generally accepted by the intellectually competent who have taken the trouble to inform themselves with an open mind. The following letter was written in response to a request to state his position, it having been alleged that he was not a believer in organic evolution:

Washington, D. C.,
29 August 1922

My Dear Professor Curtis:

May it not suffice for me to say, in reply to your letter of August 25th, that, of course, like every other man of intelligence and education, I do believe in organic evolution. It surprises me that at this late date such questions should be raised.

Sincerely yours,

Woodrow Wilson

Prof. W. C. Curtis,
Columbia, Mo.

In view of all the facts, may we not say that the present storm against organic evolution is but an expression of malign influences of prejudice and ignorance, hostile to what we may envision as the high destiny of our Western world.

Affidavit Read to the Court at Dayton, Tennessee, July 20, 1925

KIRTLEY F. MATHER

The facts of life development are so numerously displayed and so evident in the rocks of the earth's crust that every geologist with whom I am acquainted has accepted the evolutionary principle as demonstrated. Much of the exposed part of the earth's crust is composed of rocks deposited in layers as sand, mud, gravel or limestone in the seas, lakes, or ponds of past time, or upon the surface of dry land. These are in many places broken through by masses of rock which have formed by solidification of molten lava. The successive ages of the various kinds and formations of rock are determined by their physical relations. Where not greatly disturbed by crumpling or upheaval of the earth's crust, the rocks formed in layers are obviously still in their original order, the oldest underneath and the younger layers in order one upon the other, just as they may now be observed in the hills overlooking Dayton, Tennessee. Where cut through by rocks which were once in a fluid state, it is apparent that each body of rock is younger than the youngest rock through which it broke and older than the oldest rocks deposited upon its surface after it was solid. Thus the succession of physical events in the history of the earth may be determined by patient and careful scrutiny of the earth's surface as it now is visible, either in natural or artificial exposure such as canyon walls, valley slopes, mines and wells.

In many of these rocks there are found entombed the fossil remains of the animals and plants which were alive at the time the rocks were formed. Some of these are the shells or bones of animals that lived in the seas or lakes, some are the harder parts of animals that lived on the land and were buried beneath the mud of river flats or the ashes blown out of volcanic vents. Discovering these fossil remains and knowing by their physical relations the successive ages of the rocks in which they are found, the geologist is able to sketch the history of animal and plant life upon the earth.

156

At Least 100 Million Years

In the very oldest rocks which have yet been discovered, which are at least 100,000,000 years old there are absolutely no traces whatsoever of any animal or plant life. In somewhat younger rocks, but rocks also referred to the oldest era of geological history, the Archeozoic era, there are remains of one-celled plants of the type known as algae. The next era of earth history has been named the Proterozoic. In rocks formed during it, there are a very few fossils of lowly types of shell-bearing animals and some rather obscure markings which are probably in part due to the presence of worms and in part represent the remains of sea-weeds. The rocks of these two oldest eras are nearly everywhere much distorted and broken by volcanic activity and crustal upheavals.

Upon these ancient formations there rest in orderly succession the layers deposited during the several periods of time which geologists group into what is called the Paleozoic era, which began at least 50,000,000 years ago. Most of the rocks of Tennessee were laid down during that long space of time. In this state, as elsewhere, these strata are known at many places to contain a great abundance of fossils. In the oldest rocks of that era, the fossils are of many and various invertebrate animals, many of which are of kinds not now known to exist anywhere on the face of the earth today. There are no fossils of animals which had a backbone of any sort in any of these rocks. In somewhat younger beds, referred to as the second period of the Paleozoic era, there are, however, very scanty and fragmentary remains of primitive fishes, the first known animals which possessed a backbone. The oldest known forest, composed of trees of fern-like rather than of seedbearing types, was found a few years ago in New York in rocks formed about at the middle of this Paleozoic era. That was the time when fishes ruled the waters, for remains of sharks and lung-fishes are present in great numbers in the rocks formed in the seas, but in the rocks laid down on the land or in swamps there is not a trace of animals with a backbone, although insects and land snails have left their fossil remains in them. Toward the end of the Paleozoic era, however, the rocks formed of desert sands and swamps contain the footprints and petrified bones of amphibians and reptiles, the first animals with a backbone which could breathe air by means of lungs. This part of the Paleozoic system of rocks includes the coal seams of the eastern states, and associated with the coal are many beautiful specimens of ferns and primitive evergreen trees, but none of the modern types of flowering plants. At about the close of the Paleozoic era the Appalachian Mountains were formed by the crumpling of the earth's crust in this region.

That episode of crustal crumpling is taken as the milestone to mark the end of the Paleozoic and the beginning of the Mesozoic era, which began at least 25,000,000 years ago. Since that time, Tennessee and neighboring states have, with minor exceptions, remained continually above sea level, so that we have to transfer our search to other localities to find the continuation of the fossil record. The Mesozoic era, the fourth great era of earth's history, is frequently referred to as the age of reptiles. In practically all the stratified rocks of this era there are petrified bones and footprints which tell that cold-blooded, scaley animals with backbones and four limbs lived in great numbers on land, in the sea, and in the air. The largest and most ferocious animals that ever inhabited the lands left their bones among the fossils of that era. Animals with enough feathers to enable them to fly, yet with claws on their forelimbs and teeth in their jaws, lived then and indicate the transition forms between reptiles and birds. In the same rocks with those reptiles, most of which have long since vanished from the face of the earth, a very few fragments of quite primitive mammals have been found.

These are small and insignificant creatures, most of whom laid eggs as do a couple of species of small mammals today, but who suckled their young, were warm-blooded and presumably had no scales as surface covering. For the most part the reptiles were small-brained and large-bodied; they placed their trust in strength of talon and claw, rather than in mentality and agility. Observing the earth at that time, one could not help feeling that no good could possibly come from that welter of blood-thirstiness and cruelty. Yet the small minority of puny mammals, present then, was so endowed with instinct, such as parental love for offspring, that at the end of Mesozoic time it became the dominant form of life on land, while the few reptiles which did not become extinct were for the most part banished to the swamps and deserts or other out-of-the-way places. The close of Mesozoic time, the age of reptiles, was marked by the upheaval of the Rocky Mountains. In a small fraction of the time that has elapsed since then, the entire Grand Canyon of the Colorado River has been carved by the ceaseless wear of running water. For this, and many other reasons, geologists believe that each of these eras of time should be measured in terms of tens of millions of years.

The Cenozoic era, which began 5,000,000 or 10,000,000 years ago, began as the Rocky Mountains were formed. Most of the rocks of that era are still unconsolidated layers of silt or sand or volcanic ash, although some are firmly cemented into sandstone, limestone, etc. In the earliest beds deposited around the flanks of the newborn mountains of the western states, the bones of a great variety of mammals have been found. They are evidently the improved offspring of the puny mammals which had lived in constant fear of the ponderous reptiles during the preceding era. Not until about this time had there been any large quantity of the kinds of vegetation upon which modern mammals feed, and this presumably explains in part the slowness of the mammalian minority in throwing off the yoke of the reptilian majority during the age of reptiles. The first flowering plants had left their leaves and seed pods in the rocks formed during the middle of the Mesozoic era, but grasses and herbs, fruit- and nut-bearing trees were not numerous until the beginning of the Cenozoic era.

With an abundance of the right kind of plant food and freed from reptile dominion, the mammals increased rapidly in numbers, and their bones in great variety may today be seen in the rocks of the Rocky

Mountains and other regions. Among those of the earliest Cenozoic strata may be mentioned the five-toed and four-toed ancestral horses, the trunkless and small-tusked ancestral elephant, the catlike forerunner of the modern seal. At that time, too, we find the first record of a primate, that order of mammals to which the zoologists refer man. This was evidently a small quadruped with toes terminated neither in hoofs nor claws, but with rather horny nails and with teeth adapted neither for grinding grain like those of a horse nor for tearing flesh like those of a tiger nor for gnawing nuts like those of a squirrel, but like those of a man for eating herbs, fruits and eggs. But in general appearance this creature resembled a rat much more closely than a monkey, ape or man. Bones of that lowly type of primate have been found in North America, Asia and North Africa.

Somewhat higher in the series of Cenozoic strata of India, there were recently found a fragment of jaw which had teeth totally different from those of any non-primate, somewhat different from those of a monkey, and closely resembling those of the great apes and of man. That animal lived somewhere between 2,000,000 and 10,000,000 years ago. He is believed to have been ancestral to the apes, chimpanzees, gorillas and mankind, all of which had by that time become completely differentiated from the monkey strain. If that be true, man has become distinct from the other anthropoids since that creature left his bones on the banks of an Indian stream. Narrowing our attention now to the strain that leads to man, the next fossil of significant interest is that known as the ape-man of Java. Some thirty years or so ago there was found on the island of Java a partially cemented layer of gravel and sand containing fossil bones and fossil plant remains. The plants were of the same sort as found elsewhere in rocks known to have been formed rather late in the Cenozoic era just before the first glaciers of the great Ice Age were accumulating; therefore, it must be that the associated animal bones are also of that age. The skull of this animal had a brain capacity somewhat greater than that of the most brainy apes now living and somewhat less than that of the smallest-brained human tribe. He had a receding forehead and a heavy ridge of bone above his eyes like an adult chimpanzee; yet his leg bones show unmistakably that he stood and walked erect upon his hind limbs. The name ape-man describes him exactly; he was truly intermediate in body structure between the apes and man. He lived 1,000,000 or 2,000,000 years ago. In rocks of just about that same age in England there have been found crudely fashioned flint implements, unmistakably shaped by some intelligent creature with hands so developed as to be capable of holding a stone and striking it with another stone. Modern apes have been observed to hold clubs in their clumsy hands, but none of them can at will touch his thumb against the tip of each finger on the same hand. Presumably the creature who chipped the flints found in those rocks near Foxhall, England, could do so.

Then came the first of the great glacial advances of the Ice Age about 1,000,000 years ago. Five times the northern lands were buried beneath a mantel of moving ice. Five times the ice melted until the glaciers were at least as small as those now remaining in Greenland and in the valleys of Alaska. In the gravels deposited in Germany by the rivers flowing from the melting ice of either the first or the second of these interglacial intervals, there has been found the jaw of the so-called Heidelberg man. The jaw resembles that of a modern man; its sides are nearly parallel, the canine teeth are only a little higher than the incisors and molars. But it has no chin at all, and the portion of the jawbone which articulates with the skull just in front of the ears looks considerably like the equivalent portion of an ape's jaw. Scientists classify that creature as a member of the same genus to which modern man belongs, but as a different species.

Gravels of later interglacial stages have revealed the bones of still another extinct species even closer to modern man. More than a score of practically complete skeletons and hundreds of fragmentary bones of this the Neanderthal man have been found in France, Spain and Germany. It is chiefly in the characters of the skull rather than in the other bones of the skeleton that he differs from modern man. His forehead was very receding, his brain capacity was just a little less than that of the most primitive of existing savage tribes; his brow ridges were more prominent than those of the Negro, his chin was approximately half way between the chinless profile of the Heidelberg man and the clearly defined chin of the white race of today. With his petrified bones there are frequently found the stone spearheads and the bone knives which he fashioned. To this array of facts concerning him, I want to add just one inference. Many skulls of Neanderthal type were broken when found, as though struck with a hammer on top of the head either at the moment of death or very shortly thereafter. Several tribes of aborigines in recent years break the skulls of their dead in order, as they say, to permit the spirit to start on its journey to the happy hunting ground. The inference is that the Neanderthal man, a couple of hundred thousand years ago, had the same thought that man was immortal.

During the last of the glacial stages, about the same time that the ice pushed southward across Ohio and Indiana to the Ohio River, 40,000 or 50,000 years ago, there lived in southern Europe a race of men known as the Cro-Magnons. They were stalwart highbrows with prominent chins and large brain capacity, and eyebrow ridges no more protruding than those of the existing white race, but with massive cheekbones like the North American Indian. Clearly they belonged to the same species as that which today includes the white, yellow, brown and red races, but they cannot be included in any of these races. Their implements were much better manufactured than those of their predecessors, the Neanderthals, and they had a remarkable artistic ability as shown by the pictures they engraved or painted on the walls of caves in southern France. For thousands of years they maintained their life in Europe, but about 10,000 years ago they were displaced by the first members of the races of mankind which are today in existence.

During all this time no known record of the presence of man or manlike creatures was left in either North or South America. Not until the ice sheets of the latest glacial episode had dwindled nearly to disappearance was any clear indication of man's presence left in the New World. The oldest human inhabitants of North America were members of the existing races of mankind. They reached this continent not more than 10,000 or 12,000 years ago.

The facts stated in the foregoing paragraphs have been discovered by many different individuals. Probably no one man could be found who could testify to all of them as having been personally observed by himself. Knowledge of them is the common property of countless scientists. I can, however, affirm the truth of many of these facts from personal observations; the others I believe to be true because of my confidence in the technical ability and integrity of those who have seen the actual evidence. I have also studied many of the specimens collected by those fellow-workers and now on exhibition in various museums. In 1916 and 1917 I examined the oldest known rocks of the Archeozoic era in eastern Ontario and was unable to discover any fossil remains in them. The presence of these rocks had already been made known by a Canadian geologic survey party. I was accompanied by four or five of my students. In this bleak and windswept mass of rounded rock hills and impassable swamps, these ancient rocks are cleanly displayed. On the same trip I saw in slightly younger rocks of the same era in that locality the evidence of the presence of primitive organisms, but no record of any of the higher forms of life. In 1906 I collected fossil shells of lowly invertebrates from the early Paleozoic rocks of Wisconsin. During the spring of 1916 I found the remains of somewhat higher types of invertebrates in slightly younger rocks of the same era in eastern Ontario and later described these fossils in publications of the Ontario bureau of mines and in the *Ottawa Naturalist*. Other invertebrate fossils of about the same age and about the same kinds were observed when I was in Bolivia in 1919 and 1920. Accompanied by half-breed guides and camp hands I, together with K. C. Heald, formerly chief of the oil and gas section of the United States Geological Survey, pushed far beyond the outposts of civilization into the rocky vastnesses of the eastern Andes and there we found these fossil remains.

Saw Evidences in Rocks

I have seen the fossil remains of primitive fishes of middle Paleozoic age on a number of occasions near Columbus, Ohio; in 1917, in Allen County, Kentucky, and in 1919, in Sumner County, Tennessee. I observed the footprints of large reptiles in rocks formed shortly after the upheaval of the Appalachian Mountains at several places in the Connecticut Valley during 1921. While exploring in Alaska during the summer of 1923, I searched for fossils in rocks of middle Mesozoic age, but found in them only the remains of shellfish and corals. There was a party of six dispatched by the United States Geological Survey to search for mineral resources in a previously unknown and altogether uninhabited portion of the Alaska Peninsula, not far from the famed valley of Ten Thousand Smokes, so named because of the countless vents from which steam roared heavenward. We had to cut steps with our geologic hammers across glaciers and snow fields in traversing the almost inaccessible mountains of that bleak, barren and rugged land. In Colorado, during the summer of 1924, I had occasion to study the petrified bones of mammals, imbedded in flat-lying rocks of the Cenozoic age directly overlaying tilted strata of the late Mesozoic age, in which were the fossil bones of reptiles. The tilting of those beds was a part of the crustal movement which formed the Rocky Mountains; the flat layers on top of them were deposited while those mountains were being eroded.

To this summary of known facts concerning the life of the past, there might be added a multitude of other facts concerning the body structures of the various animals, the life history of the individual animal from its start as a single fertilized cell until its attainment of adult stature, etc. I have, however, personal knowledge of only a few of the facts in these fields in which I am not a specialist. While exploring the headwaters of the Amazon in Bolivia and Peru in 1919 and 1920, I lived for some time among quite uncivilized peoples, many of whom had never seen a white man. At the same time I watched the habits and examined the bodies of several different kinds of South American monkeys. I have studied with care the skeletons of many of the Asiatic apes and Old World monkeys, as they were available in various university laboratories and museums. From these studies and others I can affirm the following generalized statements: Comparing the body structure of monkeys, apes and man, it is apparent that they are all constructed upon the same plan; with only trivial exceptions every bone in the body of one has its counterpart in the body of the others. Only in details of shape, in relative size and in method and angle of articulation with their neighbors do these bones differ in the different creatures just mentioned. Monkeys have long tails; some apes have long and some have short tails; man has a vestigial tail composed generally of about four vertebrae so small and so short as to be entirely concealed in the flesh and muscles at the base of the spine. In relation to the total dimensions of the body, the brain of monkeys is quite small, that of the apes is much larger, while that of man is largest of all. This determines in large degree the contour of the head; thus the face of the monkey occupies more space than the top and back of its head, that of the apes is comparatively smaller, while the face of man is smallest of all in relation to the total area of head surface. No one would be surprised or shocked to learn that apes and monkeys had a common ancestor, nor would he regard it as a startling scientific theory, yet in general there are more differences between the modern monkeys and the modern apes, such as the chimpanzee, the gorilla, the gibbon and the orangutang than there are between the apes and man. Yet in general there are more differences between the apes and man than there are between the existing races of men. The gaps between these various groups are, however, largely filled by the fossils, some of which I have already described. There are in truth no missing links in the record which connects man with the other members of the order of primates.

Such facts as I have stated above can be explained only by the conclusion that man has been formed through long processes of progressive development, which when traced backward through successively simpler types of life, each living in more remote antiquity, lead unerringly to a single primordial cell. The facts ascertained by natural science are obviously incomplete; the record of the rocks by no means tells the whole story. Man not only has an efficient and readily adaptable body, he also possesses a knowledge of moral law, a sense of rightness, a confidence that his reasoning mind finds response in a rational universe, and a hope that his spiritual aspirations will find increasing answer in a spiritual universe. Such things as these cannot be preserved in the fossil record, yet their presence must be accounted for. Nor have we a direct record of whence came the first living cells. The inference is unmistakable that the material substances from which living cells were first constructed were previously present among the rocks and minerals of the earth. All the necessary ingredients were certainly present in the outer shell of the youthful earth of even pre-Archeozoic time. But life is something more than matter. Living creatures are characterized by vital energy, something about which we really know very little, but something which is absolutely indispensable to every living creature. T. C. Chamberlin, the dean of American geologists, closes his volume on the origin of the earth with the following sentence: "It is our personal view that what we try to reduce to the mechanistic is at the same time volitical, but whether this be so or not, the emergence of what we call the living from the inorganic, and the emergence of what we call the psychic from the physiologic, were at once the transcendent and the transcendental features of the earth's evolution." With this conclusion I am in hearty accord. I believe that life as we know it is but one manifestation of the mysterious spiritual powers which permeate the universe. The geologic factors assembled in the primitive earth provided an environment within which the spiritual could manifest itself in the material. The form which it should assume may have been largely determined by that environment; the primitive cell was the result. Thus, in truth, was man made from the dust of the ground.

Again, the record of the rocks tells nothing except by inference of the previous state of the mineral matter of which the earth is made. Several theories, varying from one another in greater or lesser detail, are now under consideration by geologists and astronomers in their attempt to understand the actual beginnings and the antecedents of the earth and its fellow planets in the solar system. So far as we now know all the planets, suns and stars within range of our telescopes are composed of the same sort of matter, reducible upon analysis to about eighty different elements, nearly all of which are present in the earth. In other words, it is a fair sample of the material substances of the entire universe. Science has not even a guess as to the original source or sources of matter. It deals with immediate causes and effects, not at all with ultimate causes and effects. For science there is no beginning and no ending; all acceptable theories of earth origin are theories of rejuvenation rather than of creation— from nothing. Indeed, there is some evidence for the prevalent view that our sun had had at least one earlier generation of planets in its train before the disturbing effect of the close approach of another star caused the reorganization of part of its matter into our present solar system. Conversely, it is probable that at some remotely distant date in the future this group of planets, on one of which we live, will be similarly destroyed by another rejuvenating disturbance and still another cycle of planetary organization may take place.

But none of these facts is really in any way disturbing to the adherent to Christianity. Not one contradicts any teaching of Jesus Christ known to me. None of them could for his teachings deal with moral law and spiritual realities. Natural science deals with physical laws and material realities. When men are offered their choice between science, with its confident and unanimous acceptance of the evolutionary principle, on the one hand, and religion, with its necessary appeal to things unseen and unprovable, on the other, they are much more likely to abandon religion than to abandon science. If such a choice is forced upon us, the churches will lose many of their best educated young people, the very ones upon whom they must depend for leadership in coming years. Fortunately, such a choice is absolutely unnecessary. To say that one must choose between evolution and Christianity is exactly like telling the child as he starts for school that he must choose between spelling and arithmetic. Thorough knowledge of each is essential to success—both individual and racial—in life.

Although it is possible to construct a mechanistic, evolutionary hypothesis which rules God out of the world, the theories of theistic evolution held by millions of scientifically trained Christian men and women lead inevitably to a better knowledge of God and a firmer faith in his effective presence in the world. For religion is founded on facts, even as is the evolutionary principle. A true religion faces the facts fearlessly, regardless of where or how the facts may be found. The theories of evolution commonly accepted in the scientific world do not deny any reasonable interpretation of the stories of divine creation as recorded in the Bible, rather they affirm that story and give it larger and more profound meaning. This, of course, depends upon what the Bible is and what the meaning and interpretation of the stories are to each individual. I have been a Bible student all of my life and ever since my college days I have been intensely concerned with the relations between science and the Bible. I have made many addresses and have written several articles upon this subject. I have many times lectured to biblical students, such as those in the Boston University School of Religious Education.

It is obvious to any careful and intelligent reader of the book of Genesis that some interpretation of its account must be made by each individual. Very evidently it is not intended to be a scientific statement of the order and method of creation. In the first chapter of Genesis we are told that man was made after the plants and the other animals had been formed, and that man and woman were both created on the same day; in the second chapter of Genesis we read that man was formed from the dust of the ground before plants and other animals were made, that trees grew until fruit was upon them, that all the animals passed in review before man to be named, and then after these events woman was made. There is obvious lack of harmony between these two biblical accounts of creation so far as details of process and order of events are concerned; they are, however, in perfect accord in presenting the spiritual truth that God is the author and the administrator of the universe. And that is the sort of truth which we find in the Bible. It is a textbook of religion, not a textbook of biology or astronomy or geology. Moreover, it is just exactly the biblical spiritual truth concerning God which rings clearly and unmistakably through every theory of theistic evolution. With it modern science is in perfect accord.

Reasons for Distrust

There are a number of reasons why sincere and honest Christians have recently come to distrust evolution. These reasons must be understood and discussed frankly before the world will believe that science and religion are not in conflict. Some of the opposition to evolutionary science results from failure to read the Bible. Too many people who loudly proclaim their allegiance to the book know very little about what it really contains. The Bible does not state that the world was made about 6,000 years ago. The date 4004 B.C. set opposite Genesis 1:1 in many versions of the Bible was placed there by Archbishop Ussher only a few centuries ago. It is a man's interpretation of the Bible; it is in the footnotes added recently: it is not a part of the book itself. Concerning the length of earth history and human history, the Bible is absolutely silent. Science may conclude that the earth is 100,000,000 or 100,000,000,000 years old; the conclusion does not affect the Bible in the silghtest degree. Or if one is worried over the progressive appearance of land, plants, animals and man on the successive six days of a "creation week," there is well-known biblical support for the scientists' contention that eons rather than hours elapsed while these things were taking place. "A day in the sight of the Lord is as a thousand years, and a thousand years as a day." Taking the Bible itself as an authority dissipates many of the difficulties which threaten to make a gulf between religion and science. The fact that the seventh day was stated to be a day of rest has no bearing upon the length of the other days. I have no doubt that the man who made that chapter of Genesis had in his mind days of twenty-four hours each, but I reserve for myself the right to make my own interpretation of the meaning of words, as does every Christian, be he literalist, trivialist or modernist.

Another of the reasons for the modern distrust of science in the religious world is the idea that evolution displaces God. Many seem to think that when the scientist enthrones evolution as the guiding principle in nature he dethrones God, that the two words are somehow synonymous, that there is not room for both and one must go. But the facts are as follows: Evolution is not a power, nor a force; it is a process, a method. God is a power, a force; he necessarily uses processes and methods in displaying His power and exerting force. Many of us believe that science is truly discovering in evolution the processes and methods which God, the spiritual power and eternal force, has used and is using now to effect His will in nature. We believe we have a more accurate and a more deeply significant knowledge of our Maker today than had the Hebrew patriarchs who thought a man could hide from God in a garden, or who believed that God could tell man an untruth. (Genesis 2:17 states that God told man he would surely die if he ate the fruit of the tree of knowledge; man ate, he did not die, God knew he would not die therefor.)

Again there is the widespread misconception that if one accepts the evolutionary process as the method which God used he will find himself in a moral dilemma. Regardless of sect or creed, all followers of Christ must accept his teaching that the law of life is love, that service to others is the true guiding principle, that self-sacrifice even to death is the best trait a man can display. To many, evolution means the survival of the fittest in the struggle for existence; and that is taken to imply that the selfish triumph, the most cruel and bloodthirsty are exalted, those who disregard others win. Obviously, this is the very anthithesis of Christianity; both principles cannot be true; one must be false. The Christian needs not be told which of the two it is. Here is a real reason for opposition to evolution; men are not driven from it by the fear of discovering that their bodies are structurally like those of apes and monkeys; it doesn't bother us to discover that we are mammals, even odorous mammals—"by the sweat of your brow must man earn food" states the Bible. It does bother us to find the implication that the law of progress has thus apparently been opposed to the love of Christ. But here are the facts. It has been my privilege as a geologist to read the record in the rocks; knowing the ages of the rocks has led to better knowledge of the Rock of Ages; I have watched the procession of life on the long road from the one-celled bit of primitive protoplasm to the present assemblage of varied creatures, including man. At times of crisis in the past it was rarely selfishness or cruelty or strength of talon and of claw that determined success or failure. Survival values at different times have been measured in different terms. Ability to breathe air by means of lungs rather than to purify the blood by means of gills meant success in escaping from the water to the land. Love of offspring and tender care for the young gave the weak and puny mammals of long ago the ability to triumph over much stronger and more powerful reptiles like the dinosaur. Especially in the strain that leads to man can we note the increasing spread of habits of co-operation, or unselfishness of love. The survival of the "fit" DOES not necessarily mean either the survival of the "fittest" or of the "fightingest." It has meant in the past, and I believe it means today and tomorrow, the survival of those who serve others most unselfishly. Even in evolution is it true that he who would save his life must lose it. Here, if nowhere else, do the facts of evolution lead the man of science to stand shoulder to shoulder with the man of religion.

Another difficulty arises from our present limitations of knowledge. If man has evolved from other forms of animal life by the continuous process of evolution it is asked how can there be any difference between him and them, how can we believe that he has an immortal soul. Again, the appeal to facts makes it clear that somehow out of the continuity of process real differences have emerged. When the cow pauses on the hillside to admire the view, when the dog ceases to bay at the moon in order to construct a system of astronomy, then and not till then will we believe that there are no differences between man and other animals. Even though we may not understand how these differences arose, the facts are there; knowledge and mystery exist side by side; mystery does not invalidate the fact. Men of science are working on those very problems. They have not learned— and may never learn how God breathed a living soul into man's body. If they discover that process, and the method used, God will still be just as great a power. In the image of God cannot refer to hands or feet, heart, stomach, lungs. That may have been the conception of Moses; it certainly was not the conception of Christ who said that God is spirit, and proclaimed that man must worship Him in truth. It is man's soul, his spirit, which is patterned after God the Spirit.

Soul, Theologian's Business

It is the business of the theologian not the scientist to state just when and how man gained a soul. The man of science is keenly interested in the matter, but he should not be blamed if he cannot answer questions here. The theologian must tell when the individual gets his soul, whether at the moment of conception, or when the unborn babe first stirs within the womb, or at the moment of birth, or at the first gleam of intelligent appraisal of his environment and how he knows this.

Men of science have as their aim the discovery of facts. They seek with open eyes, willing to recognize it, as Huxley said, even if "it sears the eyeballs." After they have discovered truth, and not till then, do they consider what its moral implications may be. Thus far, and presumably always, truth when found is also found to be right, in the moral sense of the word. Men of religion seek righteousness; finding it they also find truth. The farther along the two avenues of investigation the scientist and the theologian go, the closer together they discover themselves to be. Already many of them are marching shoulder to shoulder in their endeavor to combine a trained and reasoning mind with a faithful and loving heart in every human individual and thus to develop more perfectly in mankind the image of God. Neither the right kind of mind nor the right kind of heart will suffice without the other. Both are needed if civilization is to be saved.

As Henry Ward Beecher said, forty years ago, "If to reject God's revelation of the Book is infidelity, what is it to reject God's revelation of himself in the structure of the whole globe?" With that learned preacher, men of science agree when he stated that "the theory of evolution is the working theory of every department of physical science all over the world. Withdraw this theory, and every department of physical research would fall back into heaps of hopelessly dislocated facts, with no more order or reason or philosophical coherence than exists in a basket of marbles, or in the juxtaposition of the multitudinous sands of the seashore. We should go back into chaos if we took out of the laboratories, out of the dissecting rooms, out of the field of investigation, this great doctrine of evolution." Chaos would inevitably destroy the whole moral fabric of society as well as impede the physical progress of humankind.

Affidavit Read to the Court at Dayton, Tennessee, July 20, 1925

FAY-COOPER COLE

Anthropologists accept evolution as the most satisfactory explanation of the observed facts relating to the universe, to our world and all life on it. They hold that evidence abundantly justifies us in believing that development has been from the simple to the complex and that present forms of life, including man, have been produced from earlier existing forms, but through immense periods of time.

The field of the anthropologist is man, man's body, and man's society, and in this study he finds himself working side by side with the biologist and the geologist. For the study of man's body he has worked out a set of instruments and has selected a series of points for observation, by means of which he can accurately describe each individual of a group, the length, breadth and height of head, the facial proportions, the length of limbs and so on.

In this way the anthropologist determines the average of a group or tribe or race, and can determine its normal variation. Anything strikingly beyond the normal at once becomes the subject of inquiry to determine its cause. In addition to the mathematical description there are added observations—color of skin, shape of teeth, the form of the hair, and many others.

On man's skeleton these observations are even more exact and are so definite that given a single skull or skeleton it is possible to tell with considerable certainty the age, sex and race of the individual, while for a series of skeletons the results are definite. The skeletons tell much of man's history, for the articulation of the bones and the lines of attachment of the muscles reveal how he walked, how he held his head and many other details of his life. It also reveals the fact that man presents many variations difficult to explain without referring to similar conditions found in the animal world. To gain further light on these variations the anthropologist works with the anatomist and comparative anatomist and he quickly finds that every human being of today possesses many muscles for which there is no apparent use, such muscles are those behind the ears, those going to the tail, the platysma—a muscle going from the chin to the clavicle. These are but a few among many which today are functionless in man, but are still in use by certain animals. Going to the human embryo we find these vestiges of an earlier condition much more developed while others appear for a time and then vanish before birth. Such a case is the free tail possessed by every human embryo, a few weeks before its birth.

It is difficult to explain the presence of these useless organs in man unless we believe that sometime in his development they were in use.

This study also reveals the fact that man closely resembles certain members of the animal world in every bone and organ of his body. There are differences, but they are difference of degree rather than of kind. The animals most closely resembling man are the anthropoid apes. A careful study shows that they have specialized in their way quite as much as man has in his, so that while they are very similar it is evident that man's line of descent is not through any of these anthropoids. It does appear, however, that both man and the other primates have a common precursor, but that the anthropoids must have branched off from the common stock in very remote times. If this is true, then we might hope to find in ancient strata of the rocks some evidences of earlier forms of men, who might perhaps more closely approach the common ancestor. This is exactly the case. The geologists have established the relative age of the strata of the rocks, while the palentologists have made plain the forms of life which lived in the epochs when these strata were deposited.

In the strata laid down at the end of the Pliocene period, at least 500,000 years ago, there has been found the bones of a being which appears to be an attempt of nature toward man. In the year 1891 on the island of Java, there were found the bones of an animal which in many ways seems to be intermediate between man and the anthropoids. These bones were found in undisturbed strata, forty feet below the surface, at a point where a river had cut through the mountainside. There can be no doubt that these bones were laid down at the time that stratum was deposited, and by studying the associated fauna, consisting of many extinct animals, the age of these rocks was established. These bones were not lying together, but had been scattered over a distance of about forty-five feet by the action of the ancient river which deposited them.

These semihuman bones consisted of a skull cap, a femur and two molar teeth. The skull was very low with narrow receding forehead and heavy ridges of bone above the eyesockets, while a bony ridge extended from between the eyebrows to the top of the head approaching a condition found in the cranium of the anthropoids. The brain capacity of this individual was between 850 and 900 cubic centimeters, or a little more than half of that of modern man. On the other hand it is half as much again as that of the adult gorilla, and the special development has taken place in these regions whose high development is typical of the brain of man. Hence in this respect this being seems to stand midway between man and the highest anthropoids. The teeth approach the human type and indicate the peculiar rotary mode of mastication of the human, which is impossible in animals having interlocking canine teeth. The thigh bone is straight, indicating an upright posture and ability to run and walk, as in man. And the muscle attachments show he was a terrestrial and not an arboreal form. If, as it seems probable, these four bones belonged to the same individual, he must have been more manlike than any living ape and at the same time more apelike than any human known to us. He is known as Pithecanthropus erectus or the erect ape-man.

Another find of somewhat similar nature was made only a few months ago in Bechuanaland of South Africa by Professor Dart, of the University at Johannesburg. This find consisted of the skull of an animal well developed beyond modern anthropoids in just those characters, facial and cerebral which are to be expected in a form imtermediate between man and the anthropoids. Neither of these two beings are, of certainty, directly ancestral to man, but they do seem to indicate that nature at a very early period was making experiments toward man.

Two other fossil beings, found in the early strata of the rocks, also seem to indicate a development toward man. In the strata of the second interglacial period, probably at least 250,000 years ago, there lived a being with a massive jaw, a jaw human in every respect, except that it had no chin and the ramus or upright portion toward the socket was very broad, as in the anthropoids. This jaw is so narrow behind that it is thought the tongue could not have sufficient play to allow for articulate speech. The teeth, although very large, are essentially human with even tops, as in man, while the canines lacked the tusklike character which they still retain in the apes. This jaw was found in the year 1907 in a sand pit working near Heidelberg, Germany. It was discovered in place at a depth of nearly eighty feet and lay in association with fossil remains of extinct animals which make possible its dating in geologic time. It is difficult to picture a man from the jaw alone, but this much we can say: the mouth must have projected more than in modern man, but less than in the chimpanzee or gorilla. He had a heavy protruding face, huge muscles for mastication, essentially human teeth, and he was already far removed from his primatic ancestors with large canines. He was nearer to man than to the apes; he was further along the line of evolutionary development than Pithecanthropus, the Java ape-man, and he lived at a much later period. This being is known as the Heidelberg man.

The second of these two finds which we have mentioned occurred near Piltdown in Sussex, England. This consisted of the crushed skull of a woman and a jaw which can scarcely be distinguished from that of a chimpanzee. For a time there was much question if the two could possibly belong together, but a more recent find, which occurred about three miles distant from the first, again showed portions of the same type of skull and jaw. The skull is exceedingly thick and its capacity much less than that of modern man, but it is distinctly human, while, as indicated, the jaw approaches that of an anthropoid. Here again we seem to have an approach toward man in very ancient strata.

Toward the end of the second interglacial period in Europe at least 225,000 years ago we begin to find stone implements which give indication of having been intentionally formed and used by intelligent beings. By the third interglacial period, more than 150,000 years ago these utensils have taken on definite form and we find thousands of stone axes of crude type scattered over a large portion of central and southern Europe. We have no fossil remains of man during this third interglacial period, for he then lived in the open and it would only be by the merest chance that his skeletons might be preserved to us. But when the fourth glacial epoch spread over Europe these men were compelled to make their homes in the shelters and caves of the rocks, and here in the debris around their ancient hearths we can read the record of their home life, and from this period on for a period of at least 50,000 years, we can read the record of man's occupancy of Europe as clearly as though we were reading from the pages of a book. Fortunately for the scientists, these people buried their dead and we have preserved for us a considerable number, ranging from children to adult men and women, so there is no guessing as to the sort of man who occupied Europe at this time.

They were massively built, with long arms and short legs, in height they averaged about five feet three inches for the men and four feet ten inches for the women, or about the same as the modern Japanese. The head was long and narrow, above the eyes was a heavy bony ridge, back of which the forehead retreated abruptly, indicating rather little development of the fore brain. The nose was low and broad, the upper lip projecting, but the jaw was weak and retreating. The head hung forward on a massive chest. This we know because the foramen magnum, the opening by which the spinal cord enters the cranium, was situated further back than is the case in modern man, and the points of articulation with the bones of the neck also show conclusively that the head hung habitually forward. In all cases we find the thigh bone to be curved and this, together with the points of articulation, show that the knee was habitually bent and that this man walked in a semierect position. These people known as the Neanderthal race spread out over the western half of Europe and we now know and have excavated very large numbers of the stations in which they lived. They were men—they were human—but they were much more like the anthropoids in many respects than is modern man. They lived in Europe for a period of at least 25,000 years, probably much longer, when they were displaced by newcomers who pushed in from around the eastern end of the Mediterranean and from Asia. The newcomers known as Cro-magnon, are a much finer physical type, but so closely related to modern man that it is not necessary to describe their physical type; but it is of interest that we can study his home life, his art and his life among certain animals now extinct, for a period beginning about 20,000 years ago and extending down to the coming of modern races.

Only a few points relating to man and his history have been reviewed, but enough has been said to indicate that the testimony of man's body, of his embryological life, of his fossil remains strongly points to the fact that he is closely related to the other members of the animal world, and that his development to his present form has taken place through an immense period of time.

From the above it seems conclusive that it is impossible to teach anthropology or the prehistory of man without teaching evolution.